Centerville Library
Washington-Centerville Public Library
Centerville, Ohio

DISCARD

D1212756

honey
&
oats

honey & oats

EVERYDAY FAVORITES *baked with* WHOLE GRAINS *and* NATURAL SWEETENERS

Jennifer Katzinger

Photography by Charity Burggraaf

SASQUATCH BOOKS
SEATTLE

For Lillian

———————————————

Copyright ©2014 by Jennifer Katzinger
All rights reserved. No portion of this book may
be reproduced or utilized in any form, or by any
electronic, mechanical, or other means, without the
prior written permission of the publisher.

Printed in China

Published by Sasquatch Books

18 17 16 15 14   9 8 7 6 5 4 3 2 1

Editor: Susan Roxborough
Project editor: Michelle Hope Anderson
Design: Anna Goldstein
Photographs: Charity Burggraaf
Food styling: Julie Hopper

Library of Congress Cataloging-in-Publication
Data is available.

ISBN-13: 978-1-57061-891-8

Sasquatch Books
1904 Third Avenue, Suite 710
Seattle, WA 98101
(206) 467-4300
www.sasquatchbooks.com
custserv@sasquatchbooks.com

contents

recipe list

introduction

WRITING *HONEY & OATS* has been a very gratifying and heartening experience. More than any other book I have written, it is truly the culmination of ideas and energy from friends, family, neighbors, and associates. I had written my previous books quite privately, but *Honey & Oats* allowed me to share the creative process. It is astonishing to me how many old and new friends jumped at the opportunity to share immensely valuable insights while testing this collection of recipes.

. . . .

The seed for this book was actually planted many years ago in a phone call from my wise and savvy editor Susan Roxborough. In our conversation, Susan put forward the idea of a whole-grain baking book that uses wholesome sweeteners. She explained how she loves baking for her daughter and finds it disheartening to follow a recipe only to realize it calls for an exorbitant amount of refined sugar. As I pondered this, I envisioned amber maple syrup, golden honey, earthy brown coconut-palm crystals, and tan Sucanat. I saw my kitchen counter piled high with mounds of soft, whole-grain flours in varying hues. I realized that many of our ancient grains have become more available, and awareness of them is on the rise. I found myself deeply interested in exploring traditional favorites and altering these inspiring desserts, pastries, and breads to replace white sugar and flour with unrefined natural sweeteners and whole-grain flours that are full of nutrition and often more easily digested.

So the *Honey & Oats* research began. As I embarked on these recipes, I found that the process was very different from my other books, where I developed new gluten-free and vegan baked goods from start to finish. For this book, I feel more like a seamstress altering a dress, finding just the right whole-grain flour and sweetener to substitute in a recipe and carefully adjusting the ratios of ingredients. In the hopes of enticing a wide audience to engage in the nurturing art of baking, I tried to include recipes that were not only beloved, but also approachable and straightforward.

My affinity for baking began in childhood. I grew up as somewhat of a baking apprentice, making black bread, bran muffins, and pancakes with my dad, and pop-overs, éclairs, French breads, kuchen, cookies, pies, and cakes with my mom and grandmother. As I became a young woman, I grew more and more keen to try out new ways of healthy baking, always finding it more exciting to improve a recipe than to follow one. So writing *Honey & Oats* in many ways feels nostalgic. The recipes are ones that have been with us for generations, taking me back to my baking roots.

For those who prefer a lighter baked good or who are just wading into the world of whole-grain flours, the recipes in this book provide the option to substitute half of the whole-grain flour with all-purpose flour to create a lighter version that still retains flavor and complexity. For baked goods made with teff or buckwheat flour, which are gluten-free, there is an option to include tapioca flour to create a lighter texture.

About the

ingredients

Please store all of your whole-grain flours in resealable plastic bags in the freezer or refrigerator to ensure they stay fresh.

oats

Oats impart a chewy bite, adding texture to breads and batters. Their mild, creamy, slightly sweet flavor is also neutral enough to provide a wonderful backdrop for more assertive flavors such as fruit and chocolate.

You should check to ensure that the oats you purchase are whole grain, as some oats marketed as "old-fashioned" have had the bran removed and therefore do not offer the same level of nutrition. Though oats are naturally gluten-free, most packaged oats contain trace amounts of gluten as the result of being ground in mills that also grind grains containing gluten. However, gluten-free oats are now widely available from trusted sources such as Bob's Red Mill.

einkorn

The most ancient of all cultivated grains, einkorn is rich in both flavor and nutrients, making it an increasingly popular whole grain. This creamy pale-yellow grain is milled into a fine flour that yields a desirable smooth texture and a robust flavor that is slightly sweet and nutty.

An attractively simple plant, einkorn is the least complex of all of the varieties of wheat and has the lowest gluten content. Einkorn, like most plants, contains only two sets of chromosomes. Later variations of wheat became much more genetically complex through cross-breeding. Einkorn means "one grain" in German and as its name suggests, it has only one grain per husk. Its grains are small and have thick, tough husks which makes threshing (the removal of the inedible husks) more difficult.

The domestication of wild einkorn in the Fertile Crescent of Mesopotamia more than 12,000 years ago facilitated the shift from hunter-gather societies to agricultural communities. Einkorn use spread throughout the Middle East and Central Europe, even making its way as far south as Egypt. Significant evidence of einkorn cultivation has been found in many archaeological sites.

Einkorn use declined around 3,000 years ago when newer forms of wheat became favored for their higher yield, higher gluten content (leavened breads rise better when a higher gluten flour is used), and ease of threshing. Those very same qualities that caused einkorn to fall out of favor make it an excellent choice for farmers today. Unlike its modern counterparts, einkorn's thick husk makes it more resistant to disease and it has a deep root system making it easier to grow in natural soil using organic methods. Low levels of gluten and excellent digestibility make it a promising option for many with gluten sensitivities. Einkorn can still be found growing wild in some parts of Turkey and is currently being cultivated on a small scale in parts of Europe, the Middle East, and most recently, the United States.

The rich flavor and exceptional nutritional value of einkorn make it an obvious choice for anyone looking to create delicious, healthful baked goods. It contains high levels of vitamin A, beta-carotene, lutein (a powerful antioxidant), and riboflavin. It also has twice the protein of modern wheat and has been shown to retain more antioxidants and nutrients after processing and baking.

SUBSTITUTE ALL-PURPOSE WHOLE WHEAT FLOUR

If you don't have einkorn flour on hand, all-purpose whole wheat flour can easily be substituted for the einkorn flour in any recipe. The substitution is simply 1:1 and the end result will be remarkably similar.

wheat

The transition to whole grains in most kitchens and bakeries often begins with **WHOLE-WHEAT FLOUR.** Nutty and earthy, it is often used as a replacement for all-purpose flour. This substitution certainly works in many recipes, especially those where a chewy or grainy texture is desired. But because whole-wheat flour creates a very dense baked good with a heavy crumb, it may yield less-than-desirable results.

With a higher starch content and less gluten, finely milled **WHOLE-WHEAT PASTRY FLOUR** is often an excellent solution. It adds a slightly nutty flavor with hints of caramel without the heaviness usually associated with standard whole-wheat flour. The type of wheat used to create different flours greatly impacts their appearance and taste. Varying in hardness and protein content, each type has its own distinct flavors and baking properties. Many whole-wheat flours can have a slightly bitter aftertaste. The soft white wheat used to make whole-wheat pastry flour is lighter in color and has a mild flavor, resulting in light baked goods with a delicate crumb. Although it closely resembles regular all-purpose flour, whole-wheat pastry flour is ground with its outer, nutrient-containing layers still intact. Per serving, whole-wheat pastry flour provides 4 grams of fiber and 3 grams of protein, and contains significant levels of phosphorus, potassium, and iron.

Milled from common wheat after most or all of the germ and bran has been removed, **ALL-PURPOSE FLOUR** is a soft, finely textured, medium-gluten flour. It is made from a combination of high-gluten hard wheat and low-gluten soft wheat and can therefore be used successfully in many different types of recipes. Unbleached and bleached varieties are available: always look for unbleached, as bleached flour often contains additives that can affect its baking properties. Because only the endosperm is used and not the whole grain, all-purpose flour provides less nutrients and protein than whole-wheat or other whole-grain flours. However, any whole-grain recipe can be made lighter and airier with the addition of all-purpose flour.

barley

Mildly sweet with a subtle nut-like flavor, barley flour is a delicious and wholesome addition to many recipes. It works well in combination with wheat flours, providing a moist, tender crumb. It contains less gluten than wheat, which helps to tenderize, but still has enough gluten to allow the baked good to fully rise. In quick breads, cookies, and other recipes that do not require yeast, barley flour can be substituted for up to half of the whole-wheat or all-purpose flour and still yield excellent results.

Used by many cultures in breads, soups, stews, and alcoholic beverages, barley is one of the most prevalent cereal grains in the world and has been for thousands of years. Used by ancient Egyptians, Greeks, Hebrews, and throughout the Arab world, barley was of such importance to these ancient cultures that it often took on religious or ritualistic significance. Barley, whose wild ancestors first originated in the Fertile Crescent of Mesopotamia, is still grown widely throughout the Middle East and as far east as Tibet. Due to its hardiness and tolerance of cool climates, barley thrives in places such as Eastern and Central Europe and is especially valued in Scotland. English-, German-, and American-made beer, ale, and whiskey are all made using malted barley. Much of the barley grown in the United States is used either for animal feed or beer, but nutrient-rich barley flour is now available at many health-food stores.

Ground from barley kernels containing both the hull and the bran, whole grain barley flour contains eight essential amino acids. It is also a wonderful source of fiber and is high in protein. Be sure to look for flour that is made from whole-grain barley as its nutritional value is much greater than flour made from pearl barley (which has undergone steam processing to remove the nutrient-laden bran). Barley does contain gluten but may be tolerable for some with mild wheat-gluten intolerances.

buckwheat

Gluten-free, buckwheat is often combined with other flours that can provide rise and structure. It adds depth and complexity to baked goods with its strong, earthy, and slightly bitter flavor. It is well matched with other richly flavored ingredients, including dark chocolate, figs, and fruit.

Humans have been cultivating buckwheat for thousands of years. Originating near the Tibetan Plateau, it was one of the first crops brought to North America by Europeans and was widely grown until the early 1900s when wheat and corn, crops that responded well to nitrogen fertilizer, took center stage.

The name *buckwheat* can be misleading, as it is not a type of wheat or even a grain at all. It is actually an herbal plant related to rhubarb, with tiny pyramidal seeds that resemble beech tree nuts. (The term *buckwheat* originates from a Dutch word meaning "beech wheat.") Buckwheat seeds can be milled into flour or sold as "groats," which are the whole seeds with just the outer hull removed. In the United States, the flour is mixed with whole-wheat flour to make buckwheat pancakes; in Japan, China, and Korea, noodles are made from it; and in Russia it is used to make blini.

It is exciting to see buckwheat being used more widely again, not only for its flavor and nutritional value, but also because it is an excellent gluten-free flour option. It is very easily digested and is considered a complete protein in that it contains all eight essential amino acids. It is high in fiber as well as B vitamins and is also a wonderful source of calcium, phosphorus, and magnesium. Because it is digested slowly, you are more likely to feel very satisfied and full after eating baked goods made with buckwheat.

spelt

Mild, nutritious, and easy to bake with, spelt flour is an excellent starting point for anyone interested in using whole-grain flours. Its light flavor and high protein content (30 percent more than regular wheat) make it a good substitute for whole-wheat or all-purpose flour in many recipes. Whole spelt flour is delicious in breads and cookies, providing a grainy texture with a tender crumb. Light spelt flour has a delightfully sweet, nutty flavor and looks and performs much like regular all-purpose flour. It is even light enough to yield excellent results in pastries and cakes.

An ancestor of wheat, spelt was first cultivated in the Middle East around 5,000 to 6,000 BCE. It was first brought to the United States in the late 1800s and has become increasingly popular among organic farmers and health-food advocates for its high level of fiber, protein, calcium, and B-complex vitamins.

It should be noted that spelt is a variety of wheat; though more easily digested, it does contain gluten. Those with gluten allergies should not consume spelt, but it is reportedly tolerable for many with mild gluten sensitivities.

kamut

Smooth, golden, buttery Kamut flour is extremely versatile. It is not bitter, like many modern wheat strains, but rather slightly sweet; you can thus use less sweetener in recipes using Kamut because there is no need to mask the bitter flavor of the flour. Kamut's fine texture and mild, enjoyable flavor makes it especially well suited to pastries, cookies, or any other recipe in which butter is a key flavor.

Kamut is actually a brand name for organically grown Khorasan wheat. There are many legends surrounding its origins, including the story that it was discovered in the tombs of the Egyptian pharaohs, thus earning it the nickname "King Tut's Wheat." In 1949, an airman from Montana sent some kernels back to the States. The airman's father grew the seeds as a hobby, and in the 1970s organic farmers Mack and Bob Quinn were able to find a market for the wheat and began to grow the seeds commercially. The Quinns chose to use the name "Kamut" for their organically grown Khorasan after they discovered that it was an ancient Egyptian word for wheat.

Kamut flour is high in protein, amino acids, lipids, and minerals. Rich in complex carbohydrates, it is also an excellent source of energy and retains more of its nutrients after milling and baking than common wheat. Like spelt, Kamut does contain gluten but may be tolerated better than modern varieties of wheat by many who have gluten sensitivities.

teff

Milled from the world's smallest whole grain, teff flour has a delightfully wholesome, malty aroma; a nutty flavor; and rich, dark color. Very finely milled, teff flour provides a delicate crumb and works well to lighten heavier, denser flours. Because it is gluten-free, it is frequently used in combination with whole-wheat or all-purpose flour, which can provide rise and structure. Teff flour intensifies and deepens the flavors of the ingredients it is paired with. With hints of hazelnut and malt, it goes especially well with nuts and dried fruits.

If you have ever enjoyed Ethiopian cuisine, you have most likely eaten teff, which is native to North Africa. It is most commonly known for its use in *injera*, a traditional Ethiopian flatbread that often serves as both plate and utensil. (It is sometimes made so large that it is used as an edible tablecloth!)

Teff is a complete protein, containing all eight essential amino acids. It is especially high in lysine, an important amino acid frequently lacking in other grains. Teff flour is also rich in fiber, calcium, and copper, and contains twice as much iron as wheat.

tapioca

Tapioca flour is a starchy, slightly sweet white flour made from cassava root, which is boiled and dried, then powdered. The cassava plant is native to Brazil and can be found throughout South America. Tapioca is eaten throughout the world in various forms, including flour, flakes, sticks, and pearls; you may be most familiar with tapioca in its pearl form as used in tapioca pudding and bubble tea. The flour is often used as a thickener in pudding, pie fillings, starches, and gravies.

Gluten-free and containing no protein, tapioca does provide a small amount of folate and a fair amount of iron, as well as trace minerals. It can add body and structure to gluten-free breads—I find that using tapioca flour produces a delicious golden crust and often creates a lighter texture. It also works well to tone down and sweeten the flavors of stronger flours, making them more palatable.

honey

Using smooth, sticky, golden honey is a wonderfully natural way to add sweetness to any treat. Produced around the globe, the flavor, color, and even texture of honey varies greatly depending on the floral source from which the nectar was procured. Most often, though not always, lighter-colored honeys, such as clover, will be milder tasting, and darker-colored honeys will have a stronger flavor.

Most natural, high-quality honeys will be minimally processed and, unlike heavily processed sweeteners, still contain antioxidants and beneficial microbial properties. Raw honey is sold in its original form and never heated. Buy from farmers' markets or your local health-food store to avoid poor-quality honey tainted with antibiotics or fillers.

maple syrup

Delectably sweet and complex in flavor, maple syrup is created by boiling the sap extracted from maple trees, a process that has not changed much since it was first produced by the native peoples of North America long before Europeans arrived. Although it can be pricey, the smooth, amber-colored syrup with hints of caramel and toffee adds sweetness and depth to baked goods. It is a wonderful alternative to processed sugar, as it is minimally processed and contains significant levels of manganese and zinc, along with lower amounts of other trace minerals and vitamins.

Maple syrups labeled in the United States as grade A light amber will be thinner and have a lighter flavor. The darker-grade B, gathered later in the season, is generally thicker, with a rich and buttery flavor that is well suited for baking.

coconut palm sugar

Reminiscent of brown sugar in both taste and appearance, unrefined coconut palm sugar is quickly becoming a popular choice among food enthusiasts. A traditional sweetener used throughout Southeast Asia, coconut palm sugar is made by collecting the sap from cut flower buds of coconut palm trees. After collection, the sap is then heated to evaporate moisture; the consistency of the final product depends on how much moisture is removed from the sap. Coconut palm sugar is sold in many forms, including granules, blocks, and liquid. The granulated variation is becoming more widely available and can be found in most health-food stores.

Containing many beneficial nutrients, including B vitamins and amino acids, coconut palm sugar is also said to have a lower glycemic index than other sweeteners. Its fructose and glucose content are similar to that of cane sugar, but its minerals and enzymes help slow its absorption into the bloodstream.

sucanat

Sucanat is the most natural, least-refined sweetener made from sugar cane. It has a strong, full-bodied flavor with hints of caramel and molasses. Unlike commercial brown sugars, which are refined and then have the molasses added back in, Sucanat is made by harvesting green sugar cane, then crushing it to extract the juice. It is heated to remove excess moisture, and the resulting syrup is cooled, allowing small crystals to form. The plant's vitamins, minerals, and trace elements remain after this minimal processing, including iron, calcium, potassium, and vitamin B6.

A product of Costa Rica, Sucanat is a brand name (a contraction of "*sucre de canne naturel*"). Other similar, minimally processed products made from dried whole cane juice are panela from Latin America, *rapadura* from Brazil, muscovado from the Philippines, and jaggery from Asia, Africa, Latin America, and the Caribbean.

scones & muffins

AS A YOUNG WOMAN I had an amazing role model who was talented at any number of things, but everyone agreed Holly could make the tastiest scones. Holly was my first yoga teacher and soon became a dear friend. She and her husband, Ed, owned the juice bar below their yoga studio, where I soon began baking before heading off to school. She taught me how to look at an unbaked scone as if I were a geologist studying the earth's strata. She told me how those layers would ensure a perfect scone that baked up with a light crumb, crisp exterior, and bursts of butter throughout. She explained how important it was to cut just the right amount of cold butter into the dough, either by hand or with a food processor, until the mixture resembles small peas. While I've been baking since childhood, it is probably because of Holly that I began doing it with a passion that eventually led me to open Flying Apron Bakery with my father.

While scones and muffins are both delicious in their own right, they are very different in their overall composition. The ideal scone is biscuit-like and rich, heavier than a muffin, with an exterior slightly reminiscent of a piecrust. A muffin should be moister, soft, and cake-like.

currant pecan scones

England's Bettys Café Tea Rooms have become famous both for their exceptional teas and their exquisite baked goods. One scone I reacquaint myself with every time I visit goes by the name of Fat Rascal (perhaps because if you eat too many, you just might become one). These scones, with their burst of sweet currants and toasted pecans wrapped up in a buttery spelt dough, certainly remind me of English teatime. Serve them warm, along with a pot of piping hot tea.

MAKES 6 SCONES

→ Preheat the oven to 400 degrees F and line a baking sheet with parchment paper.

→ In a small bowl, whisk together the cream, honey, and egg. In a large bowl, combine the flour, baking powder, and salt. With a pastry blender or two knives, cut the butter into the flour mixture until it resembles coarse, pea-size crumbs. Fold in the currants and pecans. With a fork, stir the wet ingredients into the flour mixture until just combined. The dough will be crumbly.

→ Transfer the dough to a lightly floured work surface and pat it into a 6-inch circle. Cut it into 6 wedges and place them on the prepared baking sheet. Bake until golden, about 25 minutes, rotating the sheet halfway through. Let scones cool for 10 minutes before serving. Scones really taste the most delicious the day they are made. However, if you will be storing the scones for later, let the scones cool completely before placing in an airtight container. Scones will keep up to two days and are best reheated.

¾ cup cold heavy cream

¼ cup honey

1 large egg

2¼ cups whole spelt flour, or 1 cup einkorn flour and 1¼ cups whole spelt flour

2 teaspoons baking powder

1 teaspoon salt

6 tablespoons (¾ stick) cold unsalted butter, cut into small pieces

½ cup dried currants

¾ cup pecans, toasted and finely chopped

strawberry oat scones

Every year our neighbor Kathy shares her abundant harvest of strawberries. It is amazing to me because her patch does not seem large enough to yield as many berries as it does season after season. This recipe, enhanced with chewy oats, is a result of her generosity.

MAKES 8 SCONES

↬ Preheat the oven to 400 degrees F and line a baking sheet with parchment paper.

↬ In a small bowl, combine the cream and maple syrup. In a large bowl, combine the flour, oats, baking powder, salt, and nutmeg. With a pastry blender or two knives, cut the butter into the flour mixture until it resembles coarse, pea-size crumbs. Gently fold in the strawberries. With a fork, stir the wet ingredients into the flour mixture until just combined.

↬ Transfer the dough to a lightly floured work surface and knead it briefly, just until the dough comes together. Pat the dough into an 8-inch circle and cut it into 8 wedges. Place them on the prepared baking sheet. Bake until golden and slightly firm to touch, about 18 minutes, rotating the sheet halfway through. Let scones cool for 10 minutes before serving. Scones really taste the most delicious the day they are made. However, if you will be storing the scones for later, let the scones cool completely before placing in an airtight container. Scones will keep up to two days and are best reheated.

½ cup cold heavy cream

¼ cup maple syrup

1¾ cups whole-wheat pastry flour, or 1 cup einkorn flour and ¾ cups whole-wheat pastry flour

⅓ cup rolled oats

1 tablespoon baking powder

½ teaspoon salt

¼ teaspoon ground nutmeg

6 tablespoons (¾ stick) cold unsalted butter, cut into 6 pieces

1 cup chopped fresh strawberries

Measuring Tips

→ Whether you're making scones or muffins, you'll want to measure and separate your dry and wet ingredients first, have your oven preheated, and pay close attention to when the dough or batter is at the point of just holding together and requires no more mixing. Before you know it, your kitchen counter will be lined with wholesome treats baked to golden perfection, wafting smells of spices, toasted nuts, caramelized grains, and delectable healthy sweeteners.

blueberry cinnamon scones

The combination of blueberries and cinnamon is one of my favorites, especially in a fresh, tender scone. The addition of lightly toasted walnuts provides crunch, in contrast to the juicy blueberries and soft, crumbly dough.

MAKES 8 SCONES

→ Preheat the oven to 400 degrees F and line a baking sheet with parchment paper.

→ In a large bowl, combine the flour, baking powder, cinnamon, sugar, and salt. With a pastry blender or two knives, cut the butter into the flour mixture until it resembles coarse, pea-size crumbs. Gently fold in the blueberries and walnuts. Make a well in the center and pour in the cream. Briefly fold everything together until just combined.

→ Transfer the dough to a lightly floured work surface and pat it into a 7-inch circle. Cut it into 8 wedges and place them on the prepared baking sheet. Brush the tops with a little heavy cream. Bake until golden brown, about 22 minutes, rotating the sheet halfway through. Let scones cool for 10 minutes before serving. Scones really taste the most delicious the day they are made. However, if you will be storing the scones for later, let the scones cool completely before placing in an airtight container. Scones will keep up to two days and are best reheated.

2 cups barley flour, or 1 cup einkorn flour and 1 cup barley flour

1 tablespoon baking powder

1 teaspoon ground cinnamon

3 tablespoons coconut palm sugar

½ teaspoon salt

4 tablespoons (½ stick) cold unsalted butter, cut into small pieces

1 cup frozen blueberries (baked frozen)

½ cup chopped lightly toasted walnuts

1 cup cold heavy cream, plus more for brushing the scones

hazelnut date scones

These scones are sweetened with a small but notable amount of honey, which pairs nicely with the hazelnuts and dates. Their hearty texture and the inclusion of dates rather than a moist fruit make them an ideal snack for long excursions. When you head out, perhaps on a mountain hike, pack them in aluminum foil and pop them into your backpack.

MAKES 6 SCONES

¾ cup cold heavy cream

¼ cup honey

1 large egg

2¼ cups barley flour, or 1 cup einkorn flour and 1¼ cups barley flour

2 teaspoons baking powder

1 teaspoon salt

6 tablespoons (¾ stick) cold unsalted butter, cut into small pieces

½ cup chopped, pitted dates

½ cup hazelnuts, toasted and finely chopped

→ Preheat the oven to 400 degrees F and line a baking sheet with parchment paper.

→ In a small bowl, whisk together the cream, honey, and egg. In a large bowl, combine the flour, baking powder, and salt. With a pastry blender or two knives, cut the butter into the flour mixture until it resembles coarse, pea-size crumbs. Fold in the dates and hazelnuts. With a fork, stir the wet ingredients into the flour mixture until just combined. The dough will be crumbly.

→ Transfer the dough to a lightly floured work surface and pat it into a 6-inch circle. Cut it into 6 wedges and place them on the prepared baking sheet. Bake until golden, about 20 minutes, rotating the sheet halfway through. Let scones cool for 10 minutes before serving. Scones really taste the most delicious the day they are made. However, if you will be storing the scones for later, let the scones cool completely before placing in an airtight container. Scones will keep up to two days and are best reheated.

fresh-fig almond scones

Fresh figs are naturally sweet, and as they bake, their sweetness increases. These scones have a deliciously earthy flavor, with the nuttiness of the buckwheat flour and almonds interacting with the sweetness of the juicy figs and honey. Note that because buckwheat flour is gluten-free, these scones are more delicate than those made with flour containing gluten.

MAKES 8 SCONES

⇢ Preheat the oven to 400 degrees F and line a baking sheet with parchment paper.

⇢ In a small bowl, whisk together the cream, honey, and egg. In a large bowl, combine the flours, baking powder, and salt. With a pastry blender or two knives, cut the butter into the flour mixture until it resembles coarse, pea-size crumbs. Fold in the figs and almonds. With a fork, stir the wet ingredients into the flour mixture until just combined. The dough will be crumbly.

⇢ Transfer the dough to a lightly floured work surface and pat it into an 8-inch circle. Cut it into 8 wedges and place them on the prepared baking sheet. Bake until golden, about 20 minutes, rotating the sheet halfway through. Let scones cool for 10 minutes before serving. Scones really taste the most delicious the day they are made. However, if you will be storing the scones for later, let the scones cool completely before placing in an airtight container. Scones will keep up to two days and are best reheated.

¾ cup cold heavy cream

¼ cup honey

1 large egg

¾ cup buckwheat flour

1½ cups light spelt flour

2 teaspoons baking powder

1 teaspoon salt

6 tablespoons (¾ stick) cold unsalted butter, cut into small pieces

1 cup stemmed, chopped fresh figs

½ cup slivered toasted almonds

GLUTEN-FREE VARIATION: Substitute 1½ cups tapioca flour plus ¾ teaspoon xanthan gum for the light spelt flour.

Tips for Making a Superb Muffin

→ Always remember to mix the dry ingredients with the wet ingredients just until blended. This helps keep the batter light and prevents any gluten from developing that would make for a tough muffin.

→ You should spoon the muffin batter into the prepared baking cups only two-thirds full to provide adequate room for the batter to rise.

→ Once you have taken the muffins out of the oven, let them cool for 5 minutes in the baking pan, then remove them to continue cooling on a wire rack so they stay light and moist.

blueberry yogurt muffins

These moist, soft, cake-like muffins, made with a touch of honey, are absolutely lovely. A hint of lemon zest awakens the palate and interacts with the delicate Kamut flour.

MAKES 1 DOZEN MUFFINS

→ Preheat the oven to 375 degrees F and line a standard 12-cup muffin pan with paper or foil liners.

→ In a large bowl, combine the flour, baking powder, baking soda, salt, and lemon zest. Fold in the blueberries. In a medium bowl, whisk together the oil, egg, honey, and yogurt. Fold the wet ingredients into the flour mixture until just combined.

→ Divide the batter among the muffin cups, filling them two-thirds full. Bake until the muffins are golden and spring back when touched, about 25 minutes. Let them cool in the pan for 5 minutes, then transfer them to a wire rack to cool further. Serve warm or at room temperature.

2¼ cups Kamut flour, or 1 cup einkorn flour and 1¼ cups Kamut flour

1 teaspoon baking powder

1 teaspoon baking soda

½ teaspoon salt

1 teaspoon lemon zest

1 cup frozen wild blueberries (baked frozen)

½ cup canola oil

1 large egg

⅓ cup honey

1 cup plain whole-milk yogurt (my favorite is goat's milk, but all kinds work well)

raspberry oat muffins (v)

I had my first raspberry muffin when I was twelve years old at now defunct Lakeside Bakery in Kirkland, Washington. I was the busgirl there, and when there was time during my shift to take a rest, we got to choose a baked good. After that first exceptional raspberry muffin, there was no question what I would select thereafter. This recipe offers an abundance of raspberries, as well as a lot of fiber from the oats and flaxseed meal. The Kamut flour gives the muffins a lovely lift.

MAKES 1 DOZEN MUFFINS

1 cup Kamut flour, or ½ cup einkorn flour and ½ cup Kamut flour

½ cup rolled oats

½ cup flaxseed meal

1 teaspoon baking soda

¼ teaspoon salt

1 teaspoon ground cinnamon

1½ cups fresh or frozen raspberries

½ cup canola oil

½ cup water

½ cup plus 1 tablespoon maple syrup

1 teaspoon pure vanilla extract

→ Preheat the oven to 375 degrees F and line a standard 12-cup muffin pan with paper or foil liners.

→ In a large bowl, combine the flour, oats, flaxseed meal, baking soda, salt, and cinnamon. Gently fold in the raspberries. In a medium bowl, whisk together the oil, water, maple syrup, and vanilla. Fold the wet ingredients into the flour mixture until just combined.

→ Divide the batter among the muffin cups, filling them two-thirds full. Bake until the muffins are golden and spring back when touched, 25 to 30 minutes. Let the muffins cool in the pan for 5 minutes, then transfer them to a wire rack to cool further. Serve warm or at room temperature.

apple spice muffins (GF/V)

I think of these as warming winter muffins because of the spices, especially the cloves and ginger (although you could enjoy them anytime). The pumpkin adds moistness, while still offering a cake-like crumb. The little bits of apple and raisins add additional texture and sweetness.

MAKES 1 DOZEN MUFFINS

→ Preheat the oven to 350 degrees F and line a standard 12-cup muffin pan with paper or foil liners.

→ In a large bowl, combine the flour, baking soda, salt, cloves, cinnamon, nutmeg, ginger, and raisins. Add the chopped apples to the flour mixture. In a medium bowl, whisk together the oil, water, pumpkin, maple syrup, molasses, and vanilla. Fold the wet ingredients into the flour mixture until just combined.

→ Divide the batter among the muffin cups, filling them two-thirds full. Garnish each with a pecan. Bake until the muffins are golden and spring back when touched, 25 to 30 minutes. Let the muffins cool in the pan for 5 minutes, then transfer them to a wire rack to cool further. Serve warm or at room temperature.

1½ cups teff flour, or ¾ cup tapioca flour and ¾ cup teff flour

1 teaspoon baking soda

¼ teaspoon salt

⅛ teaspoon ground cloves

1 teaspoon ground cinnamon

¼ teaspoon ground nutmeg

¼ teaspoon ground ginger

½ cup raisins

⅔ cup peeled, cored, and finely chopped apple (approximately 2 small apples)

½ cup extra-virgin olive oil

½ cup water

½ cup cooked pureed pumpkin

½ cup maple syrup

1 tablespoon molasses

1 teaspoon pure vanilla extract

12 pecans, for garnish

banana buckwheat pecan muffins (GF)

These robust, pecan-filled muffins have a wonderfully tender crumb surrounding creamy pieces of banana. It is just moist enough without being overly so (as some banana muffins can be). If you prefer to substitute another liquid for the half-and-half, almond, rice, soy, or goat's milk will all work. The difference I find is that the half-and-half makes for a richer muffin and a slightly crisper top.

MAKES 1 DOZEN MUFFINS

2 cups buckwheat flour, or 1 cup tapioca flour and 1 cup buckwheat flour

1 teaspoon baking powder

1 teaspoon baking soda

½ teaspoon salt

1 teaspoon ground cinnamon

½ cup canola oil

1 large egg

1 cup half-and-half

⅓ cup coconut palm sugar

2 bananas: 1 mashed and 1 chopped

½ cup chopped lightly toasted pecans

→ Preheat the oven to 375 degrees F and line a standard 12-cup muffin pan with paper or foil liners.

→ In a large bowl, combine the flour, baking powder, baking soda, salt, and cinnamon. In a medium bowl, whisk together the oil, egg, half-and-half, coconut palm sugar, and the mashed banana. Mix the wet ingredients into the flour mixture until just combined. Fold in the chopped banana and pecans.

→ Divide the batter among the muffin cups, filling them two-thirds full. Bake until the muffins are golden and spring back when touched, 25 to 30 minutes. Let the muffins cool in the pan for 5 minutes, then transfer them to a wire rack to cool further. Serve warm or at room temperature.

pear ginger muffins with streusel topping

Fresh and ground ginger make their presence known in these gorgeously moist and pear-filled muffins. The streusel topping provides a scrumptious, crisp contrast to the moist interior. These muffins are best enjoyed warm. They make a great accompaniment to a light meal of autumn soup and soft goat cheese.

MAKES 1 DOZEN MUFFINS

⇢ Preheat the oven to 350 degrees F and line a standard 12-cup muffin pan with paper or foil liners.

⇢ To make the streusel topping, in a small bowl, mix all the ingredients with a pastry cutter or two knives until the butter is the size of small peas.

⇢ To make the muffins, in a large bowl using an electric mixer, or in the bowl of a stand mixer fitted with the paddle attachment, cream the butter with the Sucanat until fluffy, about 3 minutes. Add the egg, milk, molasses, vanilla, and fresh ginger and mix. Fold in the pears.

⇢ In a separate large bowl, combine the flour, baking powder, baking soda, salt, cinnamon, ground ginger, and cardamom. Fold the wet ingredients into the flour mixture until just combined. Scoop a little less than ½ cup of batter into each muffin cup. Sprinkle each muffin with a tablespoon of streusel topping. Bake until the muffins are golden and spring back when touched, 30 to 35 minute. Let the muffins cool in the pan for 5 minutes, then transfer them to a wire rack to cool further.

STREUSEL TOPPING:

⅓ cup barley flour

2½ tablespoons cold butter

2½ tablespoons Sucanat

¼ tablespoon ground cinnamon

Pinch of salt

6 tablespoons (¾ stick) cold butter

½ cup Sucanat

1 large egg

½ cup milk

1 tablespoon molasses

1 tablespoon pure vanilla extract

2 teaspoons peeled, grated fresh ginger

1¼ cups stemmed, cored, and chopped pears (approximately 1½ small pears)

1½ cups barley flour, or ¾ cup einkorn flour and ¾ cup barley flour

1 teaspoon baking powder

¼ teaspoon baking soda

¼ teaspoon salt

½ teaspoon ground cinnamon

¼ teaspoon ground ginger

¼ teaspoon cardamom

pineapple cranberry muffins

These zesty muffins really work well as part of a savory brunch. Pineapple and cranberries are both very acidic, and while pineapple is one of the sweetest fruits, cranberries are by far the most tart. They intermingle in this muffin in a ratio that favors the sweetness of the pineapple.

MAKES 1 DOZEN MUFFINS

→ Preheat the oven to 375 degrees F and line a standard 12-cup muffin pan with paper or foil liners.

→ In a large bowl, combine the flour, baking powder, baking soda, salt, and cinnamon. Gently fold in the cranberries, pineapple, lemon zest, and walnuts.

→ In a medium bowl, whisk together the oil, egg, honey, and yogurt. Fold the wet ingredients into the flour mixture until just blended. Divide the batter among the muffin cups, filling them two-thirds full. Bake until the muffins are golden and spring back when touched, 25 to 30 minutes. Let the muffins cool in the pan for 5 minutes, then transfer them to a wire rack to cool further. Serve warm or at room temperature.

2¼ cups light spelt flour, or 1 cup einkorn flour and 1¼ cups light spelt flour

1 teaspoon baking powder

1 teaspoon baking soda

½ teaspoon salt

1 teaspoon ground cinnamon

¼ cup chopped frozen cranberries

¾ cup chopped fresh or canned pineapple

½ teaspoon lemon zest

½ cup chopped toasted walnuts

½ cup canola oil

1 large egg

⅓ cup honey

1 cup plain whole-milk yogurt (my favorite is goat's milk, but all kinds work well)

savory spicy corn muffins

These lightly sweet, spicy muffins have a lovely golden crown and a fantastic texture that is surprisingly moist due to the chopped peppers in the batter. The toasted cumin seeds add an extra bit of pizzazz.

MAKES 1 DOZEN MUFFINS

¾ cup Kamut flour, or ½ cup einkorn flour and ¼ cup Kamut flour

¾ cup finely ground yellow cornmeal

2 teaspoons baking powder

1 teaspoon baking soda

½ teaspoon toasted cumin seeds

½ teaspoon salt

¼ cup finely chopped green onions

¼ cup finely chopped poblano chiles

1 large egg

1 cup buttermilk

1 tablespoon honey

¼ cup (½ stick) butter, melted

→ Preheat the oven to 400 degrees F and line a standard 12-cup muffin pan with paper or foil liners.

→ In a large bowl, combine the flour, cornmeal, baking powder, baking soda, cumin seeds, and salt. Stir in the green onions and chiles. In a medium bowl, whisk the egg until smooth. Whisk in the buttermilk, honey, and melted butter. Pour the wet ingredients into the flour mixture and stir until a batter forms.

→ Divide the batter among the muffin cups, filling them three-fourths full. Bake for 15 to 20 minutes, or until a wooden toothpick inserted into the center of a muffin comes out clean. Let the muffins cool in the pan for 5 minutes, then transfer them to a wire rack to cool further. Serve warm or at room temperature.

cherry corn muffins

These rich cherry muffins are sweeter than the other muffins in this chapter. Note that this batter will be darker than that of the Savory Spicy Corn Muffins (page 30) because of the teff flour.

MAKES 1 DOZEN MUFFINS

> Preheat the oven to 425 degrees F and line a standard 12-cup muffin pan with paper or foil liners.

> Combine the flours, cornmeal, baking powder, and salt in a medium bowl; make a well in the center. In a separate medium bowl, whisk together the melted butter, egg, honey, coconut palm sugar, and milk and pour the mixture into the dry ingredients. Mix the batter until just moistened; do not overmix. Fold in the cherries.

> Divide the batter among the muffin cups, filling them three-fourths full. Bake for 18 to 20 minutes, or until a wooden toothpick inserted into the center of a muffin comes out clean. Let the muffins cool in the pan for 5 minutes, then transfer them to a wire rack to cool further. Serve warm or at room temperature.

½ cup teff flour

½ cup light spelt flour

1 cup finely ground yellow cornmeal

1 tablespoon baking powder

1 teaspoon salt

½ cup (1 stick) unsalted butter, melted and cooled

1 large egg

⅓ cup honey

¼ cup coconut palm sugar

¾ cup whole milk

2 cups quartered, pitted cherries

GLUTEN-FREE VARIATION: Substitute ½ cup tapioca flour for the light spelt flour.

versatile pancakes

There is so much room for creativity with this recipe. Adding a cup of your favorite berries to the batter is delicious. (We adore blueberry pancakes at our house.) Chopped bananas are also tasty. My husband recommends dropping some dark chocolate pieces into the batter; as the pancake cooks on the skillet, the chocolate melts. This recipe can easily be doubled if you are serving a large group.

MAKES 6 LARGE PANCAKES

✢ In a large bowl, mix all the ingredients, breaking up any lumps. Pour approximately ⅓ cup ladles of the batter onto a hot griddle. Flip the pancakes when the edges appear cooked and the batter bubbles on top, about 2 minutes. Cook the pancakes for 1 more minute. Serve immediately.

FOR A TASTY DINNER, try adding sautéed vegetables to the pancake batter. My favorite savory pancake uses finely chopped onions and Swiss chard. Serve with salad or soup.

1 large egg

1 cup whole spelt flour, or ½ cup all-purpose flour and ½ cup whole spelt flour

¾ cup whole milk

1 tablespoon Sucanat

2 tablespoons canola oil

1 tablespoon baking powder

½ teaspoon salt

⅛ teaspoon ground nutmeg

Fresh fruit, yogurt, honey, or maple syrup, for serving

buttermilk biscuits

Hot biscuits fresh from the oven are a hearty treat that go with so many meals. For breakfast, drizzle them with honey and add some fresh berries. Or try them for lunch alongside a bowl of soup and a crisp salad. Of course, buttermilk biscuits smothered with your favorite gravy is a delicious American tradition.

MAKES 10 BISCUITS

2 cups Kamut flour, or 1 cup einkorn flour and 1 cup Kamut flour, sifted

¼ teaspoon baking soda

1 tablespoon baking powder

1 teaspoon salt

6 tablespoons (¾ stick) very cold unsalted butter, cut into chunks

1 cup buttermilk

→ Preheat the oven to 450 degrees F.

→ Combine the flour, baking soda, baking powder, and salt in the bowl of a food processor. Add the butter and pulse in short spurts until it resembles coarse meal—this will take just a few times. Add the buttermilk and pulse briefly just until combined. If the dough appears dry, add a splash more buttermilk. It should be a very wet dough.

→ Turn the dough out onto a lightly floured work surface. Very gently pat it until it is about ½ inch thick. Fold the dough about 5 times, then gently pat it to about a 1-inch thickness.

→ Using a biscuit cutter or the top of a glass dipped in flour, cut out 10 biscuits. Place them on a baking sheet, spacing them about ½ inch apart. Bake until light golden brown, 10 to 12 minutes.

cookies & bars

HAVING A COOKIE OR TWO every now and again is one of those simple pleasures that is best when shared with a person you love. Making a special treat for my husband, Joseph, and our daughter, Lilli, thrills me. Perhaps because she is four and new to sweets, Lilli truly appreciates the cookie experience.

Of course, it is not just any cookie that I share with my daughter. I am pretty die-hard when it comes to health, and I would have a hard time serving Lilli a typical cookie loaded with refined sugar. When compiling these recipes, in most cases I was able to decrease the amount of sweetener considerably—I even include a recipe for making your own maple-sweetened dark chocolate chips.

animal cookies (v)

These cookies are rich sans the butter. The dough is soft, pliable, and easy for kids to roll out. Be sure to have enough flour on your work surface so you can lift the cut-out cookies easily.

MAKES 2 DOZEN COOKIES

→ Preheat the oven to 350 degrees F and line 2 baking sheets with parchment paper.

→ In a large bowl using an electric mixer, or in the bowl of a stand mixer fitted with the paddle attachment, beat the oil, maple syrup, nut butter, and vanilla until smooth and creamy, about 3 minutes, scraping down the sides of the bowl occasionally. In a separate medium bowl, mix the flour, cinnamon, salt, and baking soda. With the mixer on the lowest speed, slowly add the dry ingredients. Mix until a soft dough is formed.

→ Roll the dough out on a well-floured work surface to a ¼-inch thickness. Using animal-shaped cutters, cut cookies and place them on the prepared baking sheets. Bake until the cookies are golden and firm to touch, 12 to 15 minutes, depending on the size of your cookies. Cool the cookies on the sheets on wire racks for 5 minutes, then transfer to racks or flattened paper bags to cool completely.

½ cup canola oil

½ cup plus 1 tablespoon maple syrup

¼ cup nut butter (choose your favorite)

1 teaspoon pure vanilla extract

2 cups whole-wheat pastry flour, or 1 cup einkorn flour and 1 cup whole-wheat pastry flour

1 teaspoon ground cinnamon

½ teaspoon sea salt

½ teaspoon baking soda

Tips for Perfect Cookies

→ Bring the butter to room temperature before mixing.

→ When the butter has softened, beat it with the sweetener until it is creamy and fluffy; this will produce a tender and light cookie. Note that the vegan recipes call for creaming the sweetener with oil as the oil will not turn out fluffy like butter.

→ For recipes in which you roll out the dough, the more times the dough is rerolled, the less tender your cookies will be. After four rolls, you may want to bake the remaining scraps as is.

→ Store cooled cookies in a glass jar or airtight container.

→ Cookies can be stored in airtight containers at room temperature for up to 3 days.

pecan sandies

A sandie is very similar to shortbread. The pecans, being tender and sweet on their own, enhance this buttery dough. These cookies make great winter holiday gifts and treats. They have a tendency to crumble; if you'll be mailing them in a tin, line it with parchment paper and pack them in stacks on their sides so they arrive intact.

MAKES 20 COOKIES

→ Preheat the oven to 350 degrees F.

→ In a large bowl using an electric mixer, or in the bowl of a stand mixer fitted with the paddle attachment, beat the butter and Sucanat until light and fluffy, about 3 to 4 minutes. Beat in the vanilla and salt. With the mixer on the lowest speed, gradually add the flour, mixing just until combined. Fold in the pecans.

→ Using the palms of your hands, roll the dough into 1½-inch balls. Place them on 2 ungreased baking sheets, spacing them 2 inches apart. With the slightly dampened bottom of a glass, lightly flatten each ball of dough. Bake until the cookies are golden brown, 15 to 17 minutes, rotating the sheets halfway through. Cool the cookies on the sheets on wire racks for 5 minutes, then transfer to racks or flattened paper bags to cool completely.

½ cup (1 stick) unsalted butter, at room temperature

½ cup Sucanat

1½ teaspoons pure vanilla extract

¼ teaspoon salt

1 cup Kamut flour, or ½ cup einkorn flour and ½ cup Kamut flour

1 cup pecans, coarsely chopped

shortbread cookie cutters

These delicately sweetened shortbread cookies are melt-in-your-mouth rich. My daughter and I made them in heart shapes to bring to her preschool for a Valentine's Day party. We decided to bring the cream cheese frosting (colored red and pink with beet juice) separately, so each child could decorate his or her own hearts. The kids devoured the cookies, and I felt grateful knowing their sugar intake was minimal.

MAKES 2 DOZEN COOKIES

2 cups light spelt flour, or 1 cup all-purpose flour and 1 cup light spelt flour

½ teaspoon sea salt

1 cup (2 sticks) unsalted butter

½ cup Sucanat

1 teaspoon pure vanilla extract

¼ cup half-and-half

> Preheat the oven to 350 degrees F and line 2 baking sheets with parchment paper.

> In a medium bowl, mix the flour with the salt. In a large bowl using an electric mixer, or in the bowl of a stand mixer fitted with the paddle attachment, beat the butter, Sucanat, and vanilla until smooth and creamy, about 3 minutes, scraping down the sides of the bowl occasionally. With the mixer on the lowest speed, add the dry ingredients alternately with the half-and-half in 2 additions. Mix until a soft dough is formed.

> Roll the dough out on a well-floured work surface to a ¼-inch thickness. Using your favorite-shaped cookie cutters, cut out cookies and, using a spatula, place them on the prepared baking sheets. Bake until the cookies are golden and firm to touch, 12 to 15 minutes, depending on the size of your cookies. Cool the cookies on the sheets on wire racks for 5 minutes, then transfer to racks or flattened paper bags to cool completely.

zalettis

In my twenties, I fell head over heels for this Italian cookie. The very first zalettis I baked were much sweeter; this version is full of all the flavor I originally fell for, but sweetened with just a small amount of honey. I like to have these with my afternoon espresso.

MAKES 2 DOZEN COOKIES

> In a large bowl using an electric mixer, or in the bowl of a stand mixer fitted with the paddle attachment, beat the butter and honey until smooth and creamy, about 1 minute. Add the egg, then the vanilla, beating well after each addition. In a separate large bowl, whisk together the flour, polenta, baking powder, lemon zest, rosemary, and salt. With the mixer on the lowest speed, mix the dry ingredients into the wet mixture until a soft dough is formed. Fold in the currants. Refrigerate the dough for 1 hour in a sealed container or wrapped in plastic wrap.

> Preheat the oven to 325 degrees F and line 2 baking sheets with parchment paper.

> Pinch off golf ball–size amounts of the chilled dough and roll them into balls using the palms of your hands. Place the balls on the prepared baking sheets and partially flatten each ball by pressing down gently with your hands. Bake until the cookies are golden, 12 to 15 minutes. Cool the cookies on the sheets on wire racks for 5 minutes, then transfer to racks or flattened paper bags to cool completely.

11 tablespoons (about 1⅓ stick) unsalted butter, at room temperature

½ cup honey

1 large egg at room temperature

½ teaspoon pure vanilla extract

1¾ cups whole spelt flour, or 1 cup einkorn flour and ¾ cup whole spelt flour

1 cup regular or coarse polenta

2 teaspoons baking powder

1 teaspoon lemon zest

¾ teaspoon chopped dried rosemary

¾ teaspoon salt

¾ cup dried currants or finely chopped dried sour cherries or raisins

maple-sweetened chocolate (GF)

Many regular chocolate chips and bars are sweetened with white sugar and contain less than 60 percent chocolate. I created this recipe to provide a better, healthier alternative. The maple syrup adds subtle earthy undertones. After the chocolate has solidified, you can melt it to drizzle on cakes or spread on bars, or chop it into small pieces for your own homemade chocolate "chips."

MAKES 8 OUNCES CHOCOLATE

8-ounce bar unsweetened chocolate, chopped

½ cup maple syrup

2 teaspoons pure vanilla extract

¼ teaspoon salt

→ Melt the chocolate in a double boiler or a small metal bowl set over a saucepan with a few inches of barely simmering water. (Make sure the bottom of the bowl doesn't touch the water.) Use a rubber spatula to stir the chocolate occasionally and scrape the sides of the bowl so the chocolate doesn't burn. When the chocolate is smooth and liquefied and has completely melted, whisk in the maple syrup, vanilla, and salt. Pour the chocolate into a parchment- or foil-lined container such as a 9-inch pie pan. Cover and let it sit until it has solidified, about 3 hours at room temperature or 45 minutes in the freezer. I recommend chopping the chocolate into ¼-inch squares and storing the chocolate in the freezer. Chocolate will keep for 30 days.

chocolate pecan cookies (GF)

This cocoa-rich cookie is designed for my fellow chocolate lovers. Teff flour's earthy and nutty qualities really harmonize with the flavorful chocolate in this recipe, and homemade chocolate "chips" are delectable and worth the extra work.

MAKES ABOUT 2 DOZEN COOKIES

> Preheat the oven to 350 degrees F and line 2 baking sheets with parchment paper.

> In a large bowl using an electric mixer, or in the bowl of a stand mixer fitted with the paddle attachment, beat the butter, coconut palm sugar, and maple syrup until light and fluffy, about 3 to 4 minutes. Mix in the egg and vanilla. In a separate large bowl, combine the flour, cocoa powder, baking soda, orange zest, and salt. With the mixer on the lowest speed, gradually add the dry ingredients, mixing just until combined. Fold in the chocolate chips and pecans. Refrigerate the dough in an airtight container or wrapped in plastic for 30 minutes.

> Using the palms of your hands, roll the dough into 1½-inch balls. Place them on the prepared baking sheets, spacing them 2 to 3 inches apart. Flatten the balls just a little bit, so that they remain thick. Bake cookies in batches until slightly firm to touch, 10 to 12 minutes. Cool the cookies on the sheets on wire racks for 5 minutes, then transfer to racks or flattened paper bags to cool completely.

½ cup (1 stick) butter

½ cup coconut palm sugar

½ cup maple syrup

1 large egg

1 teaspoon pure vanilla extract

1¼ cups teff flour, or ¾ cup tapioca flour and ½ cup teff flour

¼ cup cocoa powder

½ teaspoon baking soda

½ teaspoon orange zest (optional)

½ teaspoon salt

6 ounces Maple-Sweetened Chocolate (page 46) or a store-bought bittersweet chocolate bar (70% to 80% cacao), chopped into ¼-inch squares

½ cup chopped pecans

chocolate chip cookies
sans butter (v)

If you want something close to instant gratification, these vegan cookies come together rather quickly. The inclusion of almond meal adds a rich, tender texture and a nutty sweetness.

MAKES ABOUT 12 COOKIES

⅓ cup canola oil

⅓ cup maple syrup

2 teaspoons pure vanilla extract

1 cup plus 1 tablespoon light spelt flour, or ½ cup einkorn flour and ½ cup plus 1 tablespoon light spelt flour

½ cup almond meal

¼ teaspoon salt

½ teaspoon baking soda

3 ounces Maple-Sweetened Chocolate (page 46) or a store-bought bitter-sweet chocolate bar (70% to 80% cacao), chopped into chip-size morsels

→ Preheat the oven to 350 degrees F and line a baking sheet with parchment paper.

→ In a large bowl, mix the oil, maple syrup, and vanilla. In a separate large bowl, combine the flour, almond meal, salt, and baking soda. Gradually add the dry ingredients to the wet mixture, mixing just until combined. Fold in the chocolate chips.

→ Using the palms of your hands, roll the dough into 1½-inch balls. Place them on the prepared baking sheet, spacing them 2 to 3 inches apart. Gently flatten each ball of dough with your palm. Bake until the cookies are golden and slightly firm to the touch, about 10 minutes. Cool the cookies on the sheet on wire racks for 5 minutes, then transfer to racks or flattened paper bags to cool completely.

oatmeal cookies (GF)

These fiber-filled oatmeal cookies are full of juicy raisins and toasty walnuts, intermingling with a touch of buckwheat flour. The little bit of orange zest adds vibrancy. Look for certified gluten-free oats, which are now available at most grocery stores. You can make your own oat flour by pulverizing oats in a food processor or blender.

MAKES 16 COOKIES

→ Preheat the oven to 350 degrees F and line 2 baking sheets with parchment paper.

→ In a large bowl using an electric mixer, or in the bowl of a stand mixer fitted with the paddle attachment, beat the butter, maple syrup, and coconut palm sugar until light and fluffy, about 5 minutes. With the mixer on medium speed, mix in the egg and vanilla. In a separate large bowl, combine the oats, flour, flaxseed meal, baking soda, baking powder, cinnamon, and salt. With the mixer on low speed, gradually add the dry ingredients, mixing until just combined. Fold in the raisins, walnuts, and zest.

→ Using the palms of your hands, roll the dough into 1½-inch balls. Place them on the prepared baking sheets, spacing them 2 inches apart. Flatten slightly with the palm of your hand. Bake until golden, 13 to 15 minutes. Cool the cookies on the sheets on wire racks for 5 minutes, then transfer to racks or flattened paper bags to cool completely.

½ cup (1 stick) unsalted butter, at room temperature

½ cup maple syrup

1½ tablespoons coconut palm sugar

1 large egg

1 teaspoon pure vanilla extract

¾ cup rolled oats

¾ cup oat flour

½ cup buckwheat flour, or ¼ cup tapioca flour and ¼ cup buckwheat flour

½ cup flaxseed meal

½ teaspoon baking soda

½ teaspoon baking powder

¼ teaspoon ground cinnamon

¼ teaspoon coarse salt

¾ cup raisins

½ cup chopped toasted walnuts

½ teaspoon orange zest

peanut butter cookies

When I was growing up, every time my grandmother would visit, she would inevitably make apricot kuchen, pecan kuchen, and peanut butter cookies. I always helped her with the cookies: My two greatest responsibilities were pressing them with a meat tenderizer to flatten them and give them their distinct cross-hatching, and, more importantly, topping each with precisely five chocolate chips. So in this recipe, in memory of Grandma, I give you the option to add chocolate.

MAKES 2½ DOZEN COOKIES

> Preheat the oven to 300 degrees F.

> In a large bowl using an electric mixer, or in the bowl of a stand mixer fitted with the paddle attachment, cream the butter and honey until light and fluffy, about 5 minutes. With the mixer on medium speed, add the egg, peanut butter, and vanilla and mix until well combined. In a medium bowl, combine the flour, baking soda, and salt. Add the dry ingredients to the wet mixture and mix at low speed until just combined. Fold in the peanuts, raisins, and chocolate chips.

> Drop by rounded spoonfuls onto an ungreased baking sheet. Bake until the cookies are slightly brown on the edges, about 20 minutes. Cool the cookies on the sheet on wire racks for 5 minutes, then transfer to racks or flattened paper bags to cool completely.

1 cup (2 sticks) butter, at room temperature

⅔ cup honey

1 large egg

1 cup peanut butter

2 teaspoons pure vanilla extract

2 cups barley flour, or 1 cup einkorn flour and 1 cup barley flour

½ teaspoon baking soda

½ teaspoon salt

⅔ cup chopped salted peanuts

⅔ cup raisins

3 ounces Maple-Sweetened Chocolate (page 46) or a store-bought bittersweet chocolate bar (70% to 80% cacao), chopped into chip-size morsels (optional)

almond cookies

These little almond gems are sophisticated in appearance and taste while being very easy to make. The sweetened grated almonds on top are what really make these cookies special. For the holiday season, I like to cut them into diamonds rather than squares.

MAKES 2 DOZEN COOKIES

¾ cup (1½ sticks) butter

¼ cup coconut palm sugar

1 teaspoon pure almond extract

2 cups light spelt flour, or 1 cup einkorn flour and 1 cup light spelt flour

1 large egg white, lightly beaten

⅓ cup grated almonds combined with 1 tablespoon coconut palm sugar

> Preheat the oven to 350 degrees F and line 2 baking sheets with parchment paper.

> In a large bowl using an electric mixer, or in the bowl of a stand mixer fitted with the paddle attachment, cream the butter and coconut palm sugar until light and fluffy, about 4 minutes. On the lowest setting, stir in the almond. Gradually add the flour, mixing just until a tacky dough forms. Wrap the dough in plastic wrap or place in an airtight container and refrigerate for 30 minutes.

> On a lightly floured work surface, roll the dough out to about ⅛-inch thickness. Brush with the egg white and sprinkle with the almond-and-sugar mixture. Using a knife, cut the dough into ¾-inch squares. With a spatula, transfer the cookies to the prepared baking sheets. Bake until lightly golden, about 15 minutes. Cool the cookies on the sheets on wire racks for 5 minutes, then transfer to racks or flattened paper bags to cool completely.

mexican chocolate spice cookies

This recipe is by far the deepest, darkest, and most chocolaty in the book. The cinnamon and cayenne is a rich ode to Mexico.

MAKES 2 DOZEN COOKIES

4 ounces unsweetened chocolate

1 cup Kamut flour, or ½ cup einkorn flour and ½ cup Kamut flour

1 teaspoon ground cinnamon

¼ teaspoon cayenne

½ teaspoon baking powder

⅛ teaspoon salt

¾ cup (1½ sticks) butter

¾ cup coconut palm sugar

2 medium eggs

1 tablespoon pure vanilla extract

4 ounces Maple-Sweetened Chocolate (page 46) or a store-bought bittersweet chocolate bar (70% to 80% cacao), chopped

→ Preheat the oven to 375 degrees F and line 2 baking sheets with parchment paper.

→ Melt the unsweetened chocolate in a double boiler or a small metal bowl set over a saucepan with a few inches of barely simmering water. (Make sure the bottom of the bowl doesn't touch the water.) Use a rubber spatula to stir the chocolate occasionally and scrape the sides of the bowl so it doesn't burn. When the chocolate has completely melted, remove the pan from the heat and set it aside.

→ Combine the flour, cinnamon, cayenne, baking powder, and salt in a medium bowl. In a large bowl using an electric mixer, or in the bowl of a stand mixer fitted with the paddle attachment, cream the butter and coconut palm sugar, about 4 minutes. With the mixer on medium speed, add the eggs and vanilla. Then add the melted chocolate. Gradually mix in the dry ingredients on the lowest speed and fold in the chopped chocolate.

→ Drop the dough by rounded spoonfuls on the prepared baking sheets. Bake until the cookies are slightly firm to touch, 8 to 10 minutes. Cool the cookies on the sheets on wire racks for 5 minutes, then transfer to racks or flattened paper bags to cool completely.

snickerdoodles (GF)

These cinnamon gems are ideal made with teff flour. When creating this recipe, I wanted to replicate the traditional cookie, but feel free to add more Sucanat and cinnamon to amp up the flavor.

MAKES 15 COOKIES

⇢ Preheat the oven to 400 degrees F and line 2 baking sheets with parchment paper.

⇢ In a medium bowl, sift together the flour, cream of tartar, baking soda, and salt. In a large bowl using an electric mixer, or in the bowl of a stand mixer fitted with the paddle attachment, cream the butter with ½ cup and 1 tablespoon of the Sucanat on medium speed until light and fluffy, approximately 3 minutes. Scrape down the sides of the bowl. Add the egg and then the dry ingredients, beating well after each addition.

⇢ In a small bowl, combine the remaining 2 tablespoons Sucanat and the cinnamon. Using a tablespoon, form the dough into 15 balls and roll the balls in the cinnamon sugar. Place them on the prepared baking sheets, spacing them about 2 inches apart. (If you are using all teff flour, flatten the balls at this point with the palm of your hand. This is not necessary if you are substituting tapioca flour for part of the teff.) Bake until the cookies are set in the center and begin to crack, about 10 minutes, rotating the sheets after 5 minutes. Cool the cookies on the sheets on wire racks for 5 minutes, then transfer to racks or flattened paper bags to cool completely.

1⅓ cups teff flour, or ¾ cup tapioca flour and ⅓ cup plus 2 tablespoons teff flour

1 teaspoon cream of tartar

½ teaspoon baking soda

⅛ teaspoon salt

6 tablespoons (¾ stick) unsalted butter

½ cup plus 3 tablespoons Sucanat, divided

1 large egg

1 tablespoon ground cinnamon

deep, dark chocolate brownies (GF)

A bite of this rich, dark, almost fudge-like, maple-sweetened brownie with my afternoon espresso is like a sliver of paradise for me. A little bit of this intense indulgence goes a long way.

MAKES 2 DOZEN COOKIES

¾ cup (1½ sticks) cold butter, cut into pieces

4 ounces unsweetened chocolate, chopped

2 large eggs

½ cup plus 1 tablespoon coconut palm sugar

1 tablespoon molasses

½ teaspoon salt

1 teaspoon pure vanilla extract

½ cup cocoa powder

½ cup buckwheat flour, or ¼ cup tapioca flour and ¼ cup buckwheat flour

6 ounces Maple-Sweetened Chocolate (page 46) or a store-bought bitter-sweet chocolate bar (70% to 80% cacao), chopped into chip-size morsels

1 cup toasted walnuts

→ Preheat the oven to 350 degrees F. Lightly grease and flour an 11-by-7-inch baking pan.

→ Melt the butter and chocolate in a double boiler or a small metal bowl set over a saucepan with a few inches of barely simmering water. (Make sure the bottom of the bowl doesn't touch the water.) Use a rubber spatula to stir the mixture occasionally and scrape the sides of the bowl so it doesn't burn. When the chocolate and butter have completely melted, remove the pan from the heat and set it aside.

→ In a large bowl, whisk the eggs, coconut palm sugar, molasses, salt, and vanilla for a few minutes until well combined and almost foamy. Stir in the melted chocolate and butter. Gently whisk in the cocoa powder and buckwheat flour until just combined. Fold in the chopped chocolate and walnuts. Pour the batter into the prepared pan and smooth the surface evenly with a spatula. Bake until the brownies are slightly firm to touch, about 25 minutes.

date bars

This is my mother's fabulous, caramely recipe that I've adapted slightly. The date filling surrounded by a shortbread-like oat crumble is decadent—I never thought I would use the word decadent for anything other than chocolate, but I feel it is a true fit here. Note that you can use date sugar in place of the coconut palm sugar. It is less sweet and adds moisture, making the texture somewhat denser.

MAKES 3 TO 4 DOZEN BARS

→ Preheat the oven to 350 degrees F. Lightly grease a 13-by-9-inch baking pan.

→ In a medium saucepan, simmer the dates in the water for about 30 minutes, stirring frequently, until a thick paste has formed. Meanwhile, in a large bowl, combine the flour, salt, baking soda, oats, and coconut palm sugar. With a pastry cutter or two knives, cut in the butter until crumbly. Add 1 tablespoon of water and mix lightly.

→ Press half of the dough into the prepared pan. Spread the date mixture on top. Cover with the remaining dough and pat it down lightly with a spatula. Bake until the top is lightly browned, 35 to 40 minutes. Let cool for 1 hour before cutting into 1½-inch squares or 1-by-3-inch rectangles.

2½ cups pitted, chopped dates

1½ cups water

1¼ cups whole spelt flour, or ¾ cup einkorn flour and ½ cup whole spelt flour

1 teaspoon salt

½ teaspoon baking soda

1½ cups rolled oats

½ cup coconut palm sugar

½ cup (1 stick) cold butter, cut into pieces

chocolate pistachio shortbread bars

My inspiration for this recipe came from a holiday issue of Bon Appétit magazine. These cookies are quite festive: The bright-green pistachios resting atop a glistening bed of dark chocolate are truly stunning. I recommend cutting the shortbread with a hot knife wiped clean after each cut for the most striking presentation.

MAKES 2 TO 2½ DOZEN BARS

1 cup (2 sticks) butter

½ cup coconut palm sugar

½ teaspoon sea salt

2 teaspoons pure vanilla extract

1½ cups Kamut flour, or ¾ cup einkorn flour and ¾ cup Kamut flour

8 ounces Maple-Sweetened Chocolate (page 46) or a store-bought bitter-sweet chocolate bar (70% to 80% cacao), finely chopped

1 cup chopped salted pistachios

→ Preheat the oven to 375 degrees F. Line the bottom and sides of a 13-by-9-inch metal or glass baking pan with aluminum foil, leaving a 2-inch overhang around all sides. Grease the foil to prevent the shortbread from sticking.

→ In a large bowl using an electric mixer, or in the bowl of a stand mixer fitted with the paddle attachment, cream the butter, coconut palm sugar, and sea salt until light and creamy, about 5 minutes. With the mixer on medium speed, beat in the vanilla. Gradually add the flour on the lowest speed and mix well. The dough will be very sticky. Using a spatula, scrape it into the prepared pan and spread it evenly. Bake until cracked and golden, about 20 minutes. Let cool completely, about 2 hours.

→ Preheat the oven again to 375 degrees F. Scatter the chopped chocolate evenly over the shortbread. Place in the oven for 2 minutes, just long enough to melt the chocolate. With a spatula, evenly smooth the chocolate all over the cookie. Sprinkle with the pistachios and more salt if desired. Let the chocolate cool and solidify, about 20 minutes. Gripping the aluminum foil, carefully lift the shortbread out of the pan, slide it from the foil onto a cutting board, and cut into bars. I recommend cutting into 1-by-3-inch bars, but you can cut to any size you prefer.

granola bars

Tuck one of these energy bars, packed with seeds, nuts, oats, and raisins, into your bag for a meal on the go. The superb combination of crunchy and chewy textures in a subtly sweet, cookie-like bar will keep you returning to this recipe. If you want to make them gluten-free, look for oats labeled as such, sold by Bob's Red Mill and others.

MAKES 10 BARS

¾ cup rolled oats

½ cup chopped walnuts

¼ cup unsalted pumpkin seeds

½ cup whole-wheat pastry flour

½ teaspoon baking powder

¼ teaspoon salt

½ teaspoon ground cinnamon

Pinch of ground nutmeg

½ cup canola oil

⅓ cup maple syrup

1 large egg

1 teaspoon pure vanilla extract

½ cup raisins

3 ounces Maple-Sweetened Chocolate (page 46) or a store-bought bittersweet chocolate bar (70% to 80% cacao), chopped (optional)

GLUTEN-FREE VARIATION:
Substitute ½ cup oat flour, which you can make yourself by pulverizing gluten-free oats in a food processor, for the whole-wheat pastry flour.

VEGAN VARIATION:
Substitute 1½ tablespoons flaxseed meal soaked in ⅓ cup water for the egg.

→ Preheat the oven to 350 degrees F. Line an 8-inch square baking pan with aluminum foil. Be sure to leave a 1-inch overhang all around the sides of the pan. This will help you remove the granola bars.

→ Spread the oats, walnuts, and pumpkin seeds on an ungreased baking sheet and bake until they are lightly toasted, stirring every 2 to 3 minutes. This will take about 7 or 8 minutes total. Transfer to a plate to cool.

→ In a small mixing bowl, whisk together the flour, baking powder, salt, cinnamon, and nutmeg until well combined. In a large mixing bowl, stir the oil and maple syrup until smooth. Stir in the egg and vanilla, then the dry ingredients. Stir in the oat mixture until everything is well combined. Fold in the raisins and chocolate.

→ Turn the mixture out into the prepared baking pan. Press the mixture down to compact it and evenly distribute. Bake until the granola is set, 25 to 30 minutes. Place the pan on a wire rack and let the granola cool completely, about 1 hour. Gripping the aluminum foil, carefully lift the granola out of the pan, slide it from the foil onto a cutting board, and cut into bars. I recommend cutting into 1½-by-4-inch bars. You may have a small amount of granola bar left uncut; save it, as it is delicious crumbled over yogurt.

quick
breads

ONE MORNING I OPENED my front door and saw a gingham towel tucked around a steaming object. Eagerly I unfolded first one corner of the towel and then the other to reveal a fresh and still warm wedge of Irish soda bread. This generous gift came from my friend, neighbor, and now recipe tester Kathy (as she had just baked the Spotted Dog recipe that follows, for the first time). I could tell it had turned out beautifully just by looking at it. And when I tasted it, it was obvious that the spelt flour had been a great choice.

As their name implies, quick breads are quite easy to make. Because in most cases they are muffin-like, combine your ingredients gently until they are just moistened, without overmixing.

There are two quick breads with gluten-free options in this chapter. The gluten-free version of the Applesauce Currant Snack Bread is made with buckwheat flour, and the Berry Almond Breakfast Bread with teff flour. I found that these gluten-free versions required a portion of tapioca flour to bake up with a degree of lightness that would provide a pleasing experience while still being hearty. If gluten-free isn't a concern, these two recipes can still be made totally whole grain by substituting Kamut flour for the tapioca flour.

banana bread

A thick slice of banana bread warm from the oven is always a treat. The flaxseed meal, oats, and toasted walnuts enhance this tasty bread, giving it a wholesome texture and plenty of fiber. Only mildly sweet, this bread is just right for breakfast.

MAKES 1 LOAF

→ Preheat the oven to 350 degrees F and position a rack in the middle of the oven. Lightly grease and flour a 9-by-5-inch loaf pan.

→ In a large bowl, combine the flour, flaxseed meal, oats, walnuts, baking powder, baking soda, and salt. In a medium bowl, stir together the oil, coconut palm sugar, eggs, yogurt, bananas, lemon juice, and vanilla. Add the wet ingredients to the flour mixture and stir gently just until the dry ingredients are moistened. Scrape the batter into the prepared pan. Bake until a wooden toothpick inserted into the center of the loaf comes out clean, about 45 minutes. Let the bread cool in the pan for 20 minutes, then turn it out onto a wire rack to continue cooling. Serve warm or at room temperature.

1½ cups Kamut flour, or ¾ cup einkorn flour and ¾ cup Kamut flour

¼ cup flaxseed meal

¼ cup rolled oats

½ cup ground toasted walnuts

1 teaspoon baking powder

½ teaspoon baking soda

½ teaspoon salt

⅓ cup canola oil

½ cup coconut palm sugar

2 large eggs

⅓ cup plain whole-milk yogurt (I prefer goat's milk, but any will work)

1 cup mashed bananas (from about 2 medium bananas)

1 tablespoon freshly squeezed lemon juice

1 teaspoon pure vanilla extract

apricot cherry bread

When I created this recipe, I was very much inspired by the Apricot Quick Bread recipe in the Moosewood Restaurant New Classics cookbook. I am really impressed with their method for soaking oats in orange juice and oil to soften them. The first time I baked this bread, I was pleased with the outcome using light spelt flour. However, when my friend Cassandra made it with part whole spelt flour and part light spelt flour, we discovered it was equally as soft and moist, with a more satisfying structure.

MAKES 2 LOAVES

→ Preheat the oven to 350 degrees F. Lightly grease and flour two 5-by-9-inch loaf pans.

→ Place the cherries, apricots, zest, and water in a small saucepan and bring to a boil. When the water boils, immediately remove the pan from the heat and set it aside.

→ In a small bowl, combine the orange juice and oil. Stir in the oats and let them soak for 10 minutes.

→ In a large bowl, combine the flours, baking powder, baking soda, salt, cinnamon, and nutmeg. In a medium bowl, whisk together the butter, honey, eggs, and milk. Strain the water from the fruit and add it, along with the unstrained soaked oats, to the wet ingredients and stir until just combined. Divide the batter evenly between the two prepared pans. Bake until the bread is golden and firm to the touch, and a wooden toothpick inserted into the center of the loaves comes out clean, 40 to 45 minutes. Let the bread cool in the pans for 20 minutes, then turn them out onto a wire rack to continue cooling.

¾ cup dried cherries

¾ cup dried apricots, chopped

1 tablespoon freshly grated orange zest

¾ cup water

¾ cup freshly squeezed orange juice (from about 3 medium oranges)

¼ cup canola oil

¾ cup rolled oats

1¼ cups whole spelt flour

1¼ cups light spelt flour or einkorn flour

1 tablespoon baking powder

1 teaspoon baking soda

1 teaspoon salt

½ teaspoon ground cinnamon

¼ teaspoon ground nutmeg

½ cup (1 stick) butter, melted

½ cup honey

2 large eggs

1 cup whole milk

zucchini bread

As I mentioned in the introduction, my editor, Susan, was an inspiration for this book. In our conversation, Susan referred specifically to zucchini bread, where often more than a cup of white sugar is called for in just one loaf. Susan, this honey-sweetened zucchini bread is for you!

MAKES 1 LOAF

2 large eggs

½ cup canola oil

½ cup honey

2 teaspoons pure vanilla extract

1 cup grated unpeeled zucchini

1¼ cups whole-wheat pastry flour, or ¾ cup einkorn flour and ½ cup whole-wheat pastry flour

½ teaspoon baking powder

½ teaspoon baking soda

½ teaspoon salt

1 teaspoon ground cinnamon

½ teaspoon ground ginger

¼ teaspoon ground nutmeg

½ cup toasted finely chopped pecans

⅓ cup dried currants

→ Preheat the oven to 375 degrees F. Lightly grease and flour an 8-by-4-inch loaf pan.

→ In a medium bowl, whisk the eggs. Add the oil and whisk, then add the honey and vanilla and mix well. Fold in the zucchini. In a large bowl, mix the flour, baking powder, baking soda, salt, cinnamon, ginger, and nutmeg. Add the wet ingredients to the flour mixture, stirring gently just until the dry ingredients are moistened. Fold in the pecans and currants. Scrape the batter into the prepared pan. Bake until a wooden toothpick inserted into the center of the loaf comes out clean, 45 to 55 minutes. Let the bread cool in the pan for 20 minutes, then turn it out onto a wire rack to continue cooling.

pumpkin pecan bread (v)

Luscious, moderately spiced, maple-sweetened pumpkin bread, full of toasty pecans and plump sultanas is what this recipe delivers. A slice of this bread is delicious in the autumn alongside a cup of steaming chai tea.

MAKES 1 LOAF

→ Preheat the oven to 350 degrees F. Grease and flour an 8-by-4-inch loaf pan.

→ In a large bowl, combine the flour, baking powder, baking soda, salt, cinnamon, cloves, nutmeg, ginger, sultanas, and pecans. In a medium bowl, whisk together the oil, water, pumpkin, maple syrup, molasses, and vanilla. Add the wet ingredients to the flour mixture, stirring gently just until the dry ingredients are moistened. Scrape the batter into the prepared pan. Bake until loaf is golden and springs back when touched, 40 to 45 minutes. Let the bread cool in the pan for 20 minutes, then turn it out onto a wire rack to continue cooling. Serve warm or at room temperature.

1½ cups barley flour, or ¾ cup einkorn flour and ¾ cup barley flour

½ teaspoon baking powder

½ teaspoon baking soda

¼ teaspoon salt

1 teaspoon ground cinnamon

⅛ teaspoon ground cloves

¼ teaspoon ground nutmeg

¼ teaspoon ground ginger

½ cup sultana raisins

¾ cup chopped pecans

½ cup light olive oil

½ cup water

½ cup cooked pureed pumpkin

½ cup maple syrup

1 tablespoon molasses

1 teaspoon pure vanilla extract

prune pecan bread

There is a surprising ingredient in this delicately sweetened quick bread, and that is a modest amount of goat cheese. Succulent prunes folded into a smooth, honey-sweetened dough, surrounded by a sprinkling of pecans and every now and then a burst of creamy, salty cheese, bake into a very special bread. I like to serve it at lunch with a crisp green salad tossed with a simple vinaigrette.

MAKES 1 LOAF

2 cups Kamut flour, or 1 cup einkorn flour and 1 cup Kamut flour

1 teaspoon baking powder

1 teaspoon baking soda

½ teaspoon salt

½ cup (1 stick) unsalted butter, at room temperature

½ cup honey

½ teaspoon pure almond extract

2 large eggs

1 cup halved, pitted prunes

3 tablespoons goat cheese, cut into small pieces

⅓ cup toasted finely chopped pecans

→ Preheat the oven to 325 degrees F. Grease and flour a 9-by-5-inch loaf pan. Position a rack in the center of the oven.

→ In a medium bowl, whisk together the flour, baking powder, baking soda, and salt.

→ In a large bowl using an electric mixer, or in the bowl of a stand mixer fitted with the paddle attachment, cream the butter, honey, and almond extract until light and fluffy, about 3 minutes. Beat in the eggs one at a time, beating well after each addition. Set your mixer to the lowest speed and mix in the dry ingredients. Fold in the chopped prunes, goat cheese, and pecans. Spoon the batter into the prepared pan. Bake until a wooden toothpick inserted into the center of the loaf comes out clean, 55 to 60 minutes. Let the bread cool in the pan for 20 minutes, then turn it out onto a wire rack to continue cooling.

honey oat bread

If you are looking for a robust, healthy bread for sandwiches, to go with soup, or for toast in the morning, this recipe is ideal. The subtle taste of the buttermilk intermingling with the sweet hint of honey in this soft loaf makes for a very satisfying and pleasing bread.

MAKES I LOAF

1 cup plus 2 tablespoons rolled oats, divided

2¼ cups whole spelt flour, or 1 cup einkorn flour and 1¼ cups whole spelt flour

2 teaspoons baking powder

½ teaspoon baking soda

1 teaspoon salt

1 large egg

¼ cup canola oil

¼ cup honey

1¾ cups buttermilk

→ Preheat the oven to 375 degrees F. Position a rack in the middle of the oven. Thoroughly grease a 9-by-5-inch loaf pan and sprinkle it with 1 tablespoon of the oats, turning to coat the pan.

→ In a large bowl, combine the flour, baking powder, baking soda, and salt. In a medium bowl, whisk together 1 cup of the oats, egg, oil, honey, and buttermilk until well blended. Add the wet ingredients to the flour mixture, stirring gently just until the dry ingredients are moistened. Using a spatula, scrape the batter into the prepared pan, spreading it evenly to the edges. Sprinkle the remaining 1 tablespoon of oats over the top. Bake until the loaf is golden, the crust is slightly cracked, and a wooden toothpick inserted into the center of the loaf comes out clean, 40 to 50 minutes. Let the bread cool in the pan for 20 minutes, then turn it out onto a wire rack to continue cooling for about 45 minutes before slicing.

applesauce currant snack bread

This lightly sweet, moist, and delicate bread goes really nicely with homemade apple compote and a little cream. If you'd like plump currants, you can soak them in brandy or boiling water for three hours, then strain. For this recipe, I feel that making the batter with only buckwheat flour isn't an option, which is why I call for buckwheat and einkorn flours. If you don't need the gluten-free option and want to go completely whole grain, replace the buckwheat and einkorn flours with Kamut flour.

MAKES 1 LOAF

→ Preheat the oven to 350 degrees F. Grease and flour an 11-by-7-inch baking pan. Position a rack in the center of the oven.

→ In a medium bowl, whisk together the flours, baking powder, salt, cinnamon, nutmeg, and ginger. In a large bowl using an electric mixer, or in the bowl of a stand mixer fitted with the paddle attachment, beat the eggs, maple syrup, oil, and applesauce for about 3 minutes. Mix in the dry ingredients. Fold in the walnuts and currants.

→ Scrape the batter into the prepared pan. Bake until a wooden toothpick inserted into the center of the loaf comes out clean, 35 to 40 minutes. Let the bread cool in the pan for 20 minutes before slicing.

¾ cup buckwheat flour

1 cup einkorn flour

2 teaspoons baking powder

½ teaspoon salt

1 teaspoon ground cinnamon

¼ teaspoon ground nutmeg

⅛ teaspoon ground ginger

2 large eggs

⅓ cup maple syrup

⅓ cup extra-virgin olive oil

1 cup applesauce

⅔ cup chopped walnuts

½ cup dried currants

GLUTEN-FREE VARIATION: Substitute 1 cup tapioca flour for the einkorn flour.

berry almond breakfast bread

A slice of this mouthwatering bread topped with a dollop of yogurt makes for a well-rounded and satisfying breakfast. Earthy and delicate teff flour gives it a light texture akin to a coffee cake.

MAKES ONE 8-INCH COFFEE CAKE

> Position a rack in the center of the oven. Preheat the oven to 350 degrees F and grease and flour an 8-inch square pan.

> In a medium bowl, whisk together the flours, baking powder, baking soda, and salt. In a large bowl using an electric mixer, or in the bowl of a stand mixer fitted with the paddle attachment, beat the oil, coconut palm sugar, maple syrup, and vanilla, and almond. Beat in the egg. Add the dry ingredients alternately with the buttermilk in 2 additions. Fold in the berries and almonds.

> Scrape the batter into the prepared pan. Bake until a wooden toothpick inserted into the center of the bread comes out clean, 40 to 45 minutes. Let the bread cool in the pan for 20 minutes, then turn it out onto a wire rack to continue cooling.

GLUTEN-FREE VARIATION: Substitute 1 cup tapioca flour for the light spelt flour.

1 cup teff flour

1 cup light spelt flour

1 teaspoon baking powder

1 teaspoon baking soda

¼ teaspoon salt

¼ cup extra-virgin olive oil

⅓ cup coconut palm sugar

⅓ cup maple syrup

1 teaspoon pure vanilla extract

½ teaspoon pure almond extract

1 large egg

⅔ cup buttermilk

½ cup fresh blackberries

½ cup fresh raspberries

½ cup slivered almonds

sweet potato skillet corn bread

This rich, untraditional corn bread is full of character, with wheat germ, pumpkin seeds, and ample sweet potatoes. The buttermilk adds beautiful body. Just barely sweet with a hint of honey, this savory bread goes well with many dishes.

MAKES 1 LOAF

¾ cup Kamut flour, or ½ cup einkorn flour and ¼ cup Kamut flour

¼ cup wheat germ

½ cup medium-grind cornmeal

1 teaspoon baking powder

½ teaspoon baking soda

½ teaspoon coarse sea salt, plus extra for sprinkling the bread

½ cup extra-virgin olive oil

¼ cup honey

¾ cup mashed cooked sweet potato or yam (from about 1 medium sweet potato)

2 large eggs

⅓ cup buttermilk

½ cup pumpkin seeds

⇢ Position a rack in the center of the oven. Preheat the oven to 375 degrees F and lightly oil a large cast-iron skillet, and

⇢ In a medium bowl, combine the flour, wheat germ, cornmeal, baking powder, baking soda, and salt. In a large bowl using an electric mixer, or in the bowl of a stand mixer fitted with the paddle attachment, beat the oil, honey, and sweet potato. Beat in the eggs. Add the dry ingredients alternately with the buttermilk in 2 additions, mixing until just combined.

⇢ Scrape the batter into the prepared skillet and sprinkle with the pumpkin seeds and some salt. Bake until a wooden toothpick inserted into the center of the bread comes out clean, about 30 minutes. Let the bread cool in the skillet for 20 minutes before serving.

dinner bread on the fly (v)

This bread bakes up like a rustic, round Italian loaf, and because it rises with baking soda, the baking process is closer to instant gratification.

MAKES 1 ROUND LOAF

3 cups whole spelt flour, or 1½ cups
    einkorn flour and 1½ cups whole
    spelt flour
1 teaspoon sea salt
1 teaspoon baking soda
2 tablespoons maple syrup
2½ tablespoons extra-virgin olive oil
1 cup plus 1 tablespoon water

→ Preheat the oven to 375 degrees F and lightly flour a baking sheet (do not grease).

→ In a large bowl, combine the flour, salt, and baking soda. In a small bowl, combine the maple syrup, oil, and water. Mix the wet ingredients into the dry just until a smooth dough forms. On a lightly floured work surface, gently knead the bread to shape, about 3 minutes, and then form it into a 6-inch diameter round loaf.

→ Place it on the prepared baking sheet. Using a sharp knife, score it in a semicircle. Bake until golden and firm to touch, about 50 minutes. Let bread cool for 45 minutes before serving.

spotted dog (irish soda bread)

When I was growing up, my proud Irish grandma Noreen McCormick Dowd made a delicious bread that we always called Irish soda bread. It was very much like the recipe here but with all-purpose flour. In my research, I learned that true Irish soda bread does not have any sweetener, eggs, raisins, or butter, and if it does, according to Irish tradition it is called Spotted Dog or Railway Cake.

MAKES 1 LARGE LOAF

→ Preheat the oven to 450 degrees F. Lightly grease a baking sheet or cast-iron skillet.

→ In a large bowl, mix together the flour, coconut palm sugar, salt, caraway, and baking soda. With a pastry cutter or two knives, cut the butter into the dry ingredients until the mixture looks like coarse meal. Fold in the raisins.

→ In a small bowl, whisk together the egg and buttermilk. Make a well in the center of the dry ingredients and pour the egg mixture into it. Mix gently until just combined. Shape the dough into a rugged ball and transfer it to a lightly floured work surface. Knead the dough just 3 or 4 times, shaping it into an 8-inch round loaf.

→ Place the loaf on the prepared sheet. Using a sharp knife, score the bread into quarters in a crisscross pattern. The scores ought to be fairly deep, a little over 1 inch. Bake for 15 minutes, then reduce the oven temperature to 400 degrees F and bake for an additional 30 minutes, or until a wooden toothpick inserted into the center of the bread comes out clean. Let bread cool for 15 minutes before serving. Enjoy while warm.

4¼ cups whole spelt flour, or 2 cups plus 1 tablespoon einkorn flour and 2 cups plus 1 tablespoon whole spelt flour

2 tablespoons coconut palm sugar

1 teaspoon sea salt

1 tablespoon caraway seeds

1 teaspoon baking soda

¼ cup (½ stick) butter

1 cup raisins

1 large egg

1¾ cups buttermilk

yeasted breads & crackers

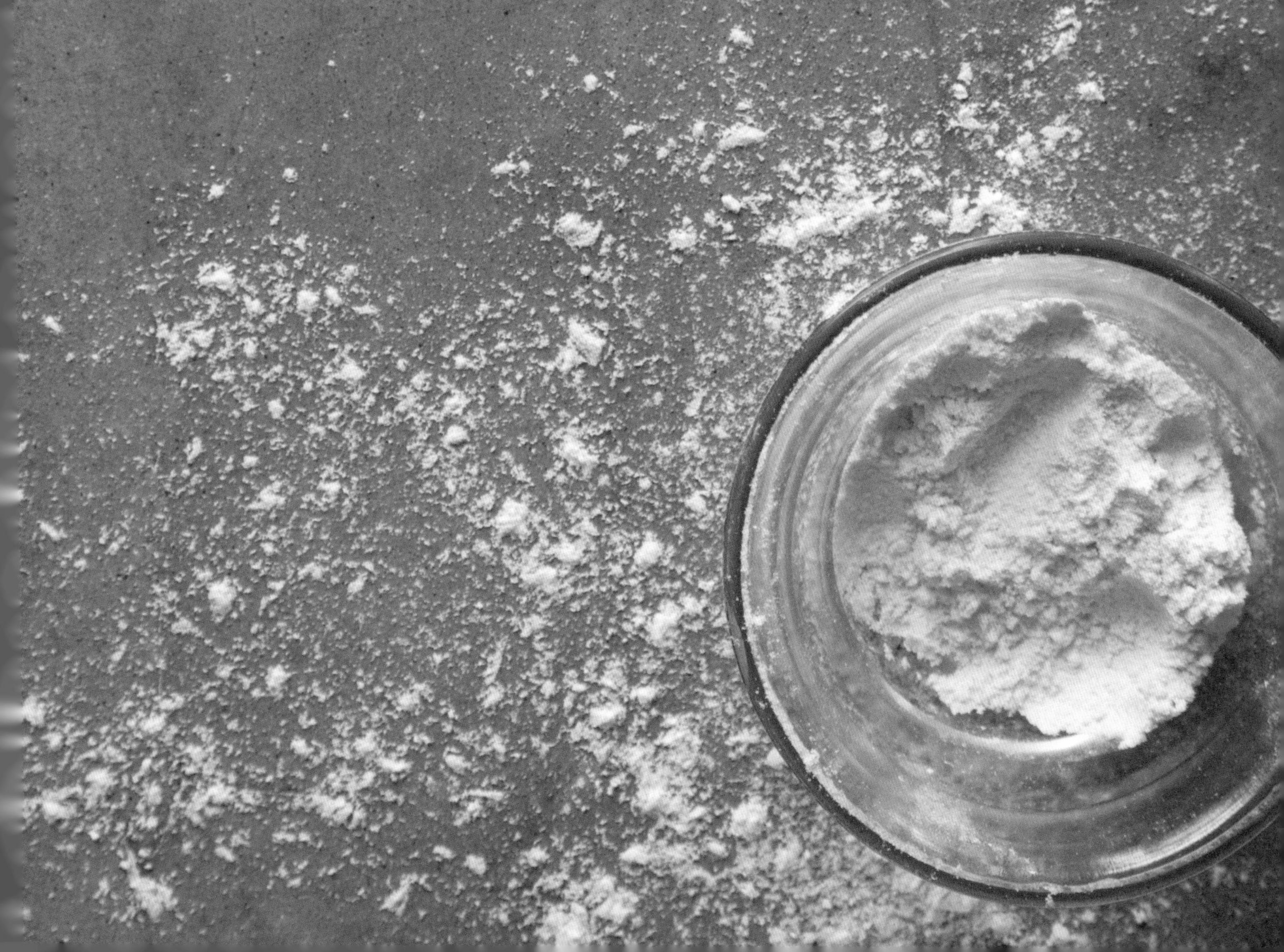

WHEN YOUR KITCHEN IS clean, and perhaps classical music is playing in the background, and you feel like nestling in and immersing yourself in the most gratifying kind of baking, then I say, bake bread! I love puttering around my home or popping out to do a bit of weeding for an hour or so as the bread rises. When I bake bread, the clock seems to slow down, and the day feels longer.

All of the recipes in this chapter are quite different from each other. The Focaccia (page 86) is the most labor intensive and takes the longest, as it must rest in the refrigerator overnight. My mother gets full credit for the Barley Walnut Boule (page 89); it rises in the fridge, allowing you to make the dough in the morning, and bake the bread upon your return from work. The Olive Oil Crackers (page 91) and Lavash Flatbread (page 95) are similar: both are large, crisp delectable flatbreads with an eye-catching presentation. The Oat-y Wheat Germ Crackers (page 93) are almost like piecrust or short-bread without the sweetness.

honey kamut bread

I like baking a loaf of this bread at the beginning of the week, as I know it will be enjoyed whole-heartedly by my family in packed lunches. This is a very rewarding bread to make; the process is straightforward and the result is deliciously mellow in flavor, with a soft crumb.

MAKES 1 LOAF

→ Combine the water, milk, oil, honey, Sucanat, and yeast in a large mixing bowl. Watch for the yeast to become activated and alive with carbon dioxide bubbles foaming at the surface of your sweet liquid mixture. Add the flour and salt in 3 additions, either by hand or on the lowest speed of your stand mixer with the dough hook attachment. Knead with a dough hook in your mixing bowl or by hand on a lightly floured work surface until the dough is smooth and elastic, about 10 to 15 minutes. Place the dough in a greased bowl and coat the top with a little oil. Cover with a clean towel and let the dough rise in a warm, draft-free place until it has doubled in size, about 50 minutes.

→ Preheat the oven to 350 degrees F. Lightly grease a 9-by-5-inch loaf pan.

→ Punch the dough down. Knead it for a few minutes until it is smooth, then form it into a loaf to fit your 9-by-5-inch loaf pan. Place the dough in the prepared pan and cover. Let rise in a warm place until almost doubled in size, about 35 minutes. Bake until golden, about 35 minutes. Let the bread cool in the pan for 10 minutes, then turn it out onto a wire rack to continue cooling.

1 cup warm water (110 to 115 degrees F)

1 tablespoon whole milk

2 tablespoons light olive oil

2 tablespoons honey

2 tablespoons Sucanat

2 teaspoons active dry yeast

3 cups Kamut flour, or 1½ cups einkorn flour and 1½ cups Kamut flour

1 teaspoon salt

Tips for Making Bread

→ It is always helpful to read the recipe from start to finish before starting to bake.

→ Check the yeast's expiration date, as it is imperative that it is fresh. Or, test a small amount of yeast by placing the yeast in warm water with a little bit of sweetener; you can tell if it is active if it begins to produce carbon dioxide bubbles.

naan

When my sister Julie and I lived close to one another as young women, we had a weekly date at a lovely neighborhood Indian restaurant. More than any curry-spiced dish, it was the warm naan that had us hooked. For those of us who do not have a tandoor (the oven in which naan is cooked), here is a recipe to create your own addictive homemade naan using your broiler. To make traditional naan, brush each baked naan with clarified butter, available at most grocery stores. It is unique butter in that the milk solids and the water have been removed from the initial butter, making for an intensified buttery taste. To make your own, melt butter in a saucepan over low heat and spoon off the white foam that rises to the surface. The golden clarified butter is what is left.

MAKES 8 TO 10 NAAN BREADS

> Sift the flour into a large bowl. Stir in the yeast, water, yogurt, egg, nigella seeds, and salt (adding more if desired) to make a soft dough. Drizzle the oil over the top. Cover the bowl with a clean kitchen towel and let the dough rest for 15 to 20 minutes. On a lightly floured surface, divide it into 8 to 10 portions and form them into balls by rolling the dough between your palms. Let the dough rest again for 20 minutes.

> Set the oven to broil. Roll each ball with a rolling pin into an oval shape. To make the ovals larger, you can toss them gently in the air like one would with pizza dough. Place 2 on a baking sheet at a time. Pop them under the broiler for 2 minutes at most, then flip them over and broil for just 30 seconds longer. The naan will be golden with air pockets crackling on their surface. Repeat with the remaining dough. As the breads are ready, brush them with clarified butter and cover with a towel on a plate until serving time. They are best enjoyed while still warm.

3 cups whole spelt flour, or 1½ cups einkorn flour and 1½ cups whole spelt flour

1½ tablespoons active dry yeast

¾ cup filtered water

2 tablespoons plain whole-milk yogurt (goat's milk or cow)

1 large egg, lightly beaten

1 teaspoon nigella seeds, crushed (optional)

2 teaspoons salt

1 tablespoon canola oil

Clarified butter, for brushing

focaccia (v)

This particular focaccia, with its herb-infused olive oil seeping into soft dimpled dough, transforms a simple meal into a spectacular one. Be sure to begin making it the day before you plan to bake, as the dough needs to rest in your refrigerator overnight.

1 LARGE FOCACCIA BREAD (SERVES 8 TO 10)

HERB OIL:

¾ cup extra-virgin olive oil

1 tablespoon chopped fresh basil

1 tablespoon chopped fresh parsley

1 tablespoon chopped fresh rosemary

1 tablespoon chopped fresh oregano

½ tablespoon chopped fresh thyme

1½ teaspoons coarse salt

½ teaspoon freshly ground black pepper

3 garlic cloves, minced

DOUGH:

2¾ cups whole spelt flour, or 1¼ cups whole wheat spelt flour and 1½ cups einkorn flour

1 teaspoon salt

1 teaspoon instant yeast

3 tablespoons extra-virgin olive oil, plus extra for greasing the pan and brushing the dough

1 cup water, at room temperature

→ To make the herb oil, in a small saucepan, heat the oil until it is just warm (about 100 degrees F). Add the herbs, salt, pepper, and garlic. Stir together, then remove the pan from the heat. Let the oil steep while you prepare the dough.

→ To make the dough, in the bowl of a stand mixer fitted with the paddle attachment, combine the flours, salt, and yeast. Add the oil and water and mix on low speed until a sticky dough comes together, about 3 minutes. Remove the paddle and replace it with the dough hook attachment. Knead the dough on medium speed for about 7 minutes, or until it is soft (it will still be sticky).

→ Using a spatula, place the dough on a well-floured work surface. Generously dust the dough with more flour while patting it into about a 6-by-3-inch rectangle. Let the dough rest for 5 minutes.

→ Coat your hands with flour and stretch the dough from each end to twice its size. Fold it, letter-style, over itself to return it to a rectangular shape. Brush the dough with oil, dust it again with flour, and loosely cover it with plastic wrap. Let the dough rest for 30 minutes. Repeat the stretching and folding process again. Again brush the dough with oil, dust with flour, and cover. After 30 minutes, repeat this one last time.

↳ Allow the covered dough to ferment on the counter for 1 hour. The dough ought to rise a bit, but it won't double in size. Line a standard baking sheet with parchment paper and grease the paper with oil, covering the entire surface. Lightly oil your hands and, using a spatula, lift the dough off the counter and transfer it to the sheet pan, keeping the rectangular shape.

↳ Spoon half of the herb oil over the dough. Using your fingertips, dimple the dough and stretch it out to fill the pan (the dough may not reach the corners)—it is important to use your fingertips only to avoid ripping the dough. Try to keep the thickness as even as possible across the focaccia. If the dough becomes too springy, let it rest for about 15 minutes and then continue dimpling. Use additional herb oil as needed to cover the entire surface. Loosely cover the pan with plastic wrap and refrigerate the dough overnight.

↳ Remove the dough from the refrigerator 3 hours prior to baking. Drizzle the remaining herb oil over the surface, pressing it down with your fingertips. Cover the pan with plastic wrap again and proof the dough at room temperature for 3 more hours, or until it doubles in size, rising to a thickness of just under 1 inch.

↳ Preheat the oven to 500 degrees F. Place the pan in the oven. Decrease the oven temperature to 450 degrees F and bake for 10 minutes. Rotate the pan 180 degrees and continue baking for 5 to 10 minutes, or until the bread is lightly golden brown. Immediately transfer the focaccia from the pan onto a cooling rack. Let it cool for 30 minutes before serving.

barley walnut boule

This hearty yet soft, round loaf makes a beautiful sandwich or dinner bread. For those of you who lead a busy lifestyle, this bread is a great choice; you can leave it to rise in your refrigerator while you are going about your day.

MAKES 2 LOAVES

→ In a large bowl, combine the flours, wheat germ, and oats. In a separate large bowl, mix 2½ cups of the flour mixture with the salt and undissolved yeast. In a small saucepan, combine the milk, water, oil, and honey over low heat. Heat until the liquid is very warm to the touch, about 120 degrees F. Gradually add the liquid to the yeast mixture, mixing well. (If you are using an electric mixer, beat 2 minutes at medium speed.) Add another cup of the flour mixture and mix thoroughly (or with the electric mixer at high speed for 2 minutes). Add the walnuts to the dough and continue adding the flour mixture in ¼ cups, stir in enough to form a stiff dough. Turn the dough out onto a lightly floured work surface and knead until smooth and elastic, about 10 minutes.

→ You have two options for rising the bread.

NO-FUSS METHOD

→ Cover the dough with plastic wrap, then a towel. Let it rest for 30 minutes.

→ Divide the dough in half. Knead it slightly and shape it into two 8-inch diameter round loaves. Place each loaf in a greased 8-inch round cake pan. Brush the loaves with oil and cover with plastic wrap. Refrigerate for at least 2 and up to 24 hours.

→ When you are ready to bake the bread, remove the dough from the refrigerator. Uncover and let it stand at room temperature for 20 minutes.

2½ cups whole spelt flour or 2½ cups einkorn flour

3 cups barley flour

½ cup wheat germ

½ cup rolled oats

4 teaspoons salt

2 packages active dry yeast

2 cups whole milk

¾ cup water

¼ cup light olive oil, plus extra for greasing the pan and brushing the dough

3 tablespoons honey

½ cup coarsely chopped walnuts

continued

TRADITIONAL METHOD

⇢ Place the dough in a greased bowl and cover it loosely with plastic wrap and a cloth towel. Let it rise in a warm place until light and doubled in size, about 1 hour.

⇢ Punch the dough down. Divide it in half. Knead it slightly and shape it into two 8-inch diameter round loaves. Place each loaf in a greased 8-inch round cake pan. Cover again with plastic wrap and a towel and let it rise for 1 hour. Uncover.

⇢ Preheat the oven to 400 degrees F. Bake until golden, about 40 minutes. Turn out the loaves from the pans immediately and cool them on wire racks.

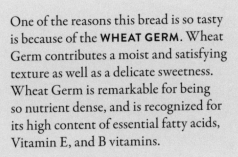

One of the reasons this bread is so tasty is because of the **WHEAT GERM**. Wheat Germ contributes a moist and satisfying texture as well as a delicate sweetness. Wheat Germ is remarkable for being so nutrient dense, and is recognized for its high content of essential fatty acids, Vitamin E, and B vitamins.

olive oil crackers (v)

Consider making these crackers as holiday gifts. I love filling big, glass mason jars with a towering stack of crackers cut into rectangles, and dressing each jar with a wide bow. Cut the dough before baking to fit whatever container or tin you choose. The crackers keep very well and are a guaranteed hit as an accompaniment to many festive appetizers.

MAKES 1 DOZEN EXTRA-LARGE CRACKERS

↯ In the bowl of a stand mixer fitted with the dough hook, whisk together the flour and salt. Add the water and oil. Mix the dough at medium speed for about 6 minutes. You can also make this dough by hand, mixing it in a large bowl and kneading it for 10 minutes on a lightly floured work surface. The dough ought to be just a little bit sticky. If it feels too dry, add a tablespoon of water; if it feels a touch too wet, add a small amount of flour, such as a tablespoon at a time.

↯ When you are finished kneading, shape the dough into a large ball, and then cut it with a floured butcher knife into 12 equal pieces. Gently rub each piece with a dab of oil, shape it into a small golf-size ball, and set it aside on a plate. Cover the plate with a cloth towel and let the dough rest at room temperature for 45 minutes.

↯ While the dough is resting, preheat the oven to 450 degrees F. Dust 4 baking sheets with flour or cornmeal.

↯ Form the crackers by flattening one dough ball at a time on a well-floured work surface. Start by flattening the ball with your hand and then rolling with a floured rolling pin back and forth in one direction until the dough is almost paper thin. This will create an attractive oblong shape that is about 5 to 6 inches long. Alternatively, you can use your pasta machine to create long, paper-thin strips. If using a pasta maker, feed the dough into the machine starting at number 1 setting and working up to the number 4 setting.

2¾ cups whole spelt flour, or 1½ cups einkorn flour and 1¼ cups whole spelt flour

1 teaspoon fine sea salt

1 cup warm water

¼ cup extra-virgin olive oil, plus more for forming crackers

Optional toppings: Salt and freshly ground black pepper, sesame seeds, caraway seeds, dried herbs

continued

→ Place the rolled-out dough on the prepared baking sheets. Poke each with the tines of a fork to prevent puffing and sprinkle on any toppings. Bake in 4 batches on baking sheets. Each sheet pan will hold 3 crackers at a time. Bake until dark golden brown, about 7 minutes, and let cool completely on wire racks before serving. Repeat the process for the remaining dough.

Marinated olives are an attractive and wonderfully flavorful accompaniment to these crackers! For a great snack, serve with soft, spreadable cheeses, such as creamy goat cheese.

oat-y wheat germ crackers

These crackers are particularly high in fiber due to the oats and wheat germ. The energy they provide is lasting, which is another reason I am so fond of these crackers. The dough is a straight-forward recipe and valuable especially around holidays, as kids really respond to food made into shapes. Halloween, Valentine's Day, Christmas, and Hanukkah, for example, can be made extra healthy and festive with crackers instead of cookies.

MAKES 15 CRACKERS

→ Preheat the oven to 350 degrees F and line 1 baking sheet with parchment paper.

→ In the bowl of a stand mixer fitted with the paddle attachment, combine the oil, butter, Sucanat, and water. On the lowest speed, mix in the flour, oats, wheat germ, and salt, until a soft dough forms, about 4 minutes. Turn the dough out onto an unfloured work surface and roll it out to ⅛ inch thickness using your rolling pin. If the dough sticks, sprinkle a light sprinkling of oats onto the work surface and on top of dough. Cut into shapes using your favorite cookie cutters. You can reroll the dough scraps to make additional crackers. Transfer cut-out dough with the aid of a spatula to the prepared sheet. Bake until golden brown, 13 to 15 minutes. Cool the crackers on wire racks.

5 tablespoons extra-virgin olive oil

⅓ cup butter

1 tablespoon Sucanat

3½ tablespoons water

¾ cup Kamut flour, or ½ cup einkorn flour and ¼ cup Kamut flour

½ cup rolled oats

¾ cup wheat germ

½ teaspoon salt

lavash flatbread (v)

This traditional Middle Eastern flatbread is becoming a very popular bread in my neighborhood. I passed this bread around on a sunny afternoon outside our house, and the neighborhood loved it! The inspiration behind this flatbread came from Hot Bread Kitchen's lavash cracker recipe in Food & Wine magazine. For my variation, I recommend using a spice called za'atar. Za'atar is a blend of dried herbs and spices and most often contains sumac, sesame seeds, thyme, and sea salt. Za'atar may vary on the inclusion or exclusion of oregano, coriander, marjoram, cumin, and savory depending on its origin, whether Middle Eastern or Mediterranean. Za'atar can be purchased at specialty food stores or online at MySpiceSage.com.

MAKES 3 LARGE FLATBREADS

2¼ teaspoons active dry yeast

1¼ cups lukewarm water, divided

4 cups whole spelt flour, or 2 cups einkorn flour and 2 cups whole spelt flour

¼ cup extra-virgin olive oil

2 tablespoons maple syrup

1½ teaspoons sea salt

1 teaspoon coarse salt, for sprinkling

1 tablespoon za'atar

1 tablespoon sesame seeds

1 teaspoon crushed coriander seeds

1 tablespoon poppy seeds

> In the bowl of a stand mixer fitted with the dough hook, combine the yeast with 2 tablespoons of the water and let sit for two minutes. Add the flour, oil, maple syrup, salt, and the rest of the water and mix on medium-low speed until a firm dough forms, about 18 minutes. Turn the dough out onto a lightly floured work surface and divide it into thirds. Let the dough rest for 15 minutes.

> Preheat the oven to 325 degrees F. Flip over three 15-by-12-inch rimmed baking sheets and lightly oil their back sides.

> On a well-floured surface, roll out the dough into 3 rectangles slightly larger than the baking sheets. They will be about ⅛ inch thick. Should the dough spring back, let it rest for a few minutes before rolling again. Drape each rectangle over a prepared baking sheets so the rolled-out rectangles hang over the pan's edges.

> Sprinkle the pieces of rolled-out dough with water, then sprinkle each piece with ½ teaspoon of the coarse salt, za'atar, and the sesame, crushed coriander, and poppy seeds. Leave the dough whole or, using a pastry wheel, cut it into twelve 3-by-5-inch pieces to make large, precut pieces. Place the pieces onto the three baking sheets and put 1 pan of lavash on each rack for 35 to 40 minutes. Rearrange the baking sheets halfway through baking by turning 180 degrees and switching baking shelves. The lavash will be browned and crisp when ready. Transfer the baking sheets to racks and let cool. When cool, break lavash into large pieces and serve.

pies
&
tarts

THE CHERISHED PIE HAS been part of our history for more than four centuries. Thankfully, the recipes have improved since then, as the original piecrusts were more utilitarian, serving specifically as a container to hold, more often than not, a savory filling. Present-day piecrust, all the more delicate, is capable of encasing a filling, but to a lesser degree, and while it's much more tasty, it is less sturdy.

In this chapter, I provide four options for crusts. The fourth, being a press-in nut crust, serves specifically for tarts or cream-filled pies. The other three crusts differentiate themselves from one another in subtle but noteworthy ways. The Butter Pastry Dough (page 99) is the least sweet and can be used for any recipe. The Butter Almond Dough (page 100) is a tad sweeter because of the inclusion of almond meal and a ½ teaspoon more sweetener. The French Pastry Dough (page 102) is the sweetest, and provides a slightly richer backdrop for the pie filling.

butter pastry dough

This flaky, tender, rich crust is a superb choice to surround any pie filling. Made with Kamut flour, it is light in color and texture. Kamut's subtle inherent sweetness really shines here.

MAKES ENOUGH FOR ONE 9-INCH SINGLE- OR DOUBLE-CRUST PIE

→ In a food processor, combine the flour, coconut palm sugar, and salt. Pulse a few times to blend. Evenly distribute the butter over the dry ingredients. Pulse (starting and stopping the motor) until the mixture resembles small peas, about 6 or 7 pulses, each lasting 3 seconds. Transfer the mixture to a medium bowl. Sprinkle the ice water onto the pastry 1 tablespoon at a time and blend in with a fork after each addition until the dough comes together. The dough will be crumbly.

→ Turn the dough out onto a lightly floured work surface and mound it with your hands. Divide the mound into 2 equal portions and form each portion into a disk roughly 5 inches in diameter. Wrap each disk in plastic wrap and refrigerate for 2 hours to chill and firm the dough.

PREBAKED CRUST FOR THE BANANA (PAGE 118) AND CHOCOLATE CREAM (PAGE 119) PIES:

→ After fitting the pastry to the pie plate, freeze the crust for at least a half hour, until chilled. Preheat the oven to 350 degrees F. When the piecrust is chilled, line it with parchment paper or aluminum foil. Fill it at least two-thirds full with pie weights, beans, or rice. Bake for 20 minutes. Remove the crust from the oven and allow it to cool for 5 minutes before removing the pie weights. Poke small holes in the bottom of the pie with the tines of a fork. Return the pie shell to the oven without the weights and bake for 10 more minutes. Cool completely before filling. You can freeze any remaining pastry for up to 30 days if it is wrapped well. When you are ready to use it, thaw the wrapped dough in the refrigerator; it will take 1 to 2 days.

FOR A SINGLE-CRUST PIE:

1 cup plus 1½ tablespoons Kamut flour, or ½ cup einkorn flour and ½ cup plus 1½ tablespoons Kamut flour

½ teaspoon coconut palm sugar

½ teaspoon salt

½ cup (1 stick) plus 1 tablespoon cold butter, cut into ¼-inch-thick pieces

3 to 4 tablespoons ice water

FOR A DOUBLE-CRUST PIE:

2¼ cups Kamut flour, or 1 cup einkorn flour and 1¼ cups Kamut flour

1 teaspoon coconut palm sugar

1 teaspoon salt

1 cup (2 sticks) plus 2 tablespoons cold butter, cut into ¼-inch-thick pieces

6 to 8 tablespoons ice water

butter almond dough

Almond undertones enhance this rich pastry. The light spelt flour makes for a delicate texture with a sound structure. The almond flour doesn't just contribute flavor, it also adds a fine and subtle consistency.

MAKES ENOUGH FOR ONE 9-INCH SINGLE- OR DOUBLE-CRUST PIE

FOR A SINGLE-CRUST PIE:

1 cup plus 1 tablespoon light spelt flour, or ½ cup einkorn flour and ½ cup plus 1 tablespoon light spelt flour

¼ cup almond flour

1 teaspoon coconut palm sugar

½ teaspoon salt

½ cup (1 stick) cold butter, cut into ¼-inch-thick pieces

3 to 4 tablespoons ice water

FOR A DOUBLE-CRUST PIE:

2¼ cups light spelt flour, or 1 cup einkorn flour and 1¼ cups light spelt flour

½ cup almond flour

2 teaspoons coconut palm sugar

1 teaspoon salt

1 cup (2 sticks) cold butter, cut into ¼-inch-thick pieces

6 to 8 tablespoons ice water

→ In a food processor, combine the flours, coconut palm sugar, and salt. Pulse a few times to blend. Evenly distribute the butter over the dry ingredients. Pulse (starting and stopping the motor) until the mixture resembles small peas, about 6 or 7 pulses, each lasting 3 seconds. Transfer the mixture to a medium bowl. Sprinkle the ice water onto the pastry 1 tablespoon at a time, blending with a fork after each addition. The dough will be crumbly.

→ Turn the dough out onto a lightly floured work surface and mound it with your hands. Divide the mound into 2 equal portions and form each portion into a disc roughly 5 inches in diameter. Wrap each disk in plastic wrap and refrigerate for 2 hours to chill and firm the dough.

Tips for Flour and Butter

→ To **MEASURE FLOUR**, scoop it into your measuring cup, slightly overfilling it. Next, use a butter knife to level the excess off the top of the cup before using the flour in your recipe.

→ When making piecrusts or pastry, always work with very cold butter. Chop it into ¼-inch-thick pieces.

→ When combining the butter and flour, **CUT IN THE BUTTER** with a pastry cutter or your food processor, pulsing the ingredients in short intervals just until you have little balls that are about the size of a pea. Then add the wet ingredients and combine just until your dough holds together. This will make for the flakiest and most tender crusts.

french pastry dough

This dough is a splash sweeter than the other doughs in this book. The recipe is for a double-crust pie. If you find that you just love this sweeter crust and want to use it for single-crust recipes as well, you can either halve the recipe or freeze the extra crust, well wrapped, for up to a month. When you are ready to use it, thaw it in the refrigerator; it will take one to two days.

MAKES ENOUGH FOR A 9-INCH DOUBLE-CRUST PIE

2¾ cups whole-wheat pastry flour, or 1½ cups einkorn flour and 1¼ cups whole-wheat pastry flour

3 tablespoons coconut palm sugar

1½ teaspoons salt

1 cup (2 sticks) cold butter, cut into ¼-inch-thick pieces

1 large egg

1 teaspoon white vinegar

¼ cup water

→ In a food processor, combine the flour, coconut palm sugar, and salt. Pulse a few times to blend. Evenly distribute the butter over the dry ingredients. Pulse (starting and stopping the motor) until the mixture resembles small peas, about 6 or 7 pulses, each lasting 3 seconds. In a large bowl, combine the egg, vinegar, and ¼ cup water. Mix in the dry ingredients with a fork. If mixture is too dry, add 1 more tablespoon of water or more as needed. The dough will be crumbly.

→ Turn the dough out onto a lightly floured work surface and mound it with your hands. Divide the mound into 2 equal portions and form each portion into a disc roughly 5 inches in diameter. Wrap each disk in plastic wrap and refrigerate for 2 hours to chill and firm the dough.

press-in almond crust (GF/V)

I just love how easily this crust comes together and how satisfying and decadent the end result is. It is ideal for tarts and cream-filled pies. Its flavor is fantastic, subtly sweet but not intense. The texture is cookie-like.

MAKES ENOUGH FOR A 9-INCH SINGLE-CRUST PIE

→ Preheat the oven to 350 degrees F. In a food processor, pulse all of the ingredients into a fine meal, being careful not to over-process so you don't end up with almond butter. Press the dough into the pan—clean, damp hands will prevent the dough from sticking to you. Bake until the crust is golden and firm to the touch, and smells like toasty almonds, about 15 minutes. Let the crust cool completely before filling.

2 cups almond flour

2 tablespoons coconut oil

2 tablespoons maple syrup

1 teaspoon pure vanilla extract

Pinch of salt

plum blackberry galette

Make this beautiful deep-purple galette toward the end of summer, when plums and blackberries are ripe for the picking. Rustic galettes have their own free-form elegance. The way the fruit is arranged in concentric circles creates an alluring visual effect.

MAKES ONE 12-INCH ROUND GALETTE

Butter Pastry Dough (page 99) for a
  single-crust pie

¼ cup plus 1 tablespoon coconut palm
  sugar, divided

1½ teaspoons arrowroot

3 large fresh plums, pitted and cut
  into 16 slices total

1 cup (½ pint) fresh blackberries

¼ cup fruit juice–sweetened preserves, preferably peach or apricot

→ Preheat the oven to 375 degrees F.

→ Roll the dough out on a well-floured sheet of parchment paper to about a 12-inch round. Slide a rimless baking sheet underneath the parchment.

→ In a medium bowl, combine ¼ cup of the coconut palm sugar and the arrowroot and toss with the plums and blackberries. Let this sit for about 30 minutes, stirring occasionally until the fruit releases its juices. Strain the fruit into a medium bowl, reserving the juice. Arrange the fruit in concentric circles on top of the dough, leaving a 3-inch space around the edge. Drizzle the reserved juice over the fruit.

→ Fold 2 inches of the dough over the galette to create a border around the fruit (the fruit should remain uncovered). Sprinkle the remaining 1 tablespoon of coconut palm sugar over the fruit.

→ Bake the galette (with the parchment) until the crust is golden brown and the filling is bubbling at the edges, about 55 minutes. Use a large spatula or the bottom of a tart pan to loosen the galette from the parchment paper and transfer it to a serving platter.

→ In a small heavy saucepan, over low heat, warm the preserves until melted, about 5 minutes. Strain into a small bowl, then brush the strained preserves over the top of the baked galette. Serve warm or at room temperature.

Tips for Working With Pie Dough

→ **TO ROLL OUT THE DOUGH**, on a well-floured work surface, place one of the chilled dough discs. Place your rolling pin, dusted with flour, in the center of the disc. Push the rolling pin away from the center. Rotate your dough continuously and dust the rolling pin and surface with more flour as needed.

→ **TO TRANSFER THE DOUGH TO THE PIE PLATE**, fold it into quarters, place the corner of the dough in the center of the plate, and unfold. Fit the dough to your pan. If you are new to making pies, you may prefer to roll out the dough on well-floured parchment paper, and rather than fold the dough into quarters to transfer it, simply flip the rolled-out dough into your pie plate, peel back the parchment, and proceed.

→ **TO FLUTE THE PASTRY**, pinch the dough between your thumb and index finger. Begin by resting the thumb and index finger of whichever hand you predominantly use on a spot on the crust's edge, with the tip of your thumb and finger on the inside perimeter. Place your index finger in between your nondominant thumb and the other index finger on the outside of the pie. Now pull the dough by moving your nondominant index finger toward the center of the pie about ¼ inch as your thumb and other index finger simultaneously pull the dough toward the outside of the pie ¼ inch. A simpler but also delightful design to finish the edge is to use a floured fork and press the dough down gently to form a pattern with the tines. A spoon pressed facedown to create a *V*-like shape is also a cute option.

apricot cherry crostata

On a summer evening, bring this crostata on a picnic with friends. It packs up easily on a sheet pan covered with foil or even transferred to the bottom of a tart pan and then wrapped up snuggly. The baked sweet and slightly tart cherries and apricots ooze their juices over crisp and tender almond pastry.

MAKES ONE 13-INCH ROUND CROSTATA

8 fresh apricots

Butter Almond Dough (page 100) for a single-crust pie

2 tablespoons light spelt flour

¼ cup coconut palm sugar, divided

1 cup (8 ounces) pitted, halved fresh cherries

¼ cup fruit juice–sweetened apricot preserves

⇢ Preheat the oven to 400 degrees F.

⇢ Fill a medium saucepan with water and bring to a boil. Prepare a bowl of ice water and set it aside. Cook the apricots in the boiling water until soft, about 1 to 2 minutes. With a slotted spatula, remove apricots to the bowl of ice water. After they have cooled, about 5 minutes, peel, halve, and pit them. Cut each apricot half into 3 wedges.

⇢ Roll the dough out on a well-floured sheet of parchment paper to a 13-inch round. Slide a rimless baking sheet underneath the parchment. Combine the flour with 1 tablespoon of the coconut palm sugar and sprinkle over the dough.

⇢ Arrange the apricot slices, rounded side down, on the dough, leaving a 3-inch space around the edge. Arrange the cherries over and around the apricot slices. Sprinkle 2 tablespoons of coconut palm sugar over the fruit.

⇢ Fold 2 inches of the dough over the crostata to create a border around the fruit (the fruit should remain uncovered) and sprinkle with the remaining tablespoon of coconut palm sugar.

⇢ Bake until the apricots are tender, about 50 minutes.

⇢ In a small heavy saucepan, over low heat, warm the preserves until melted, about 5 minutes. Strain into a small bowl, then brush the strained preserves over the top of the crostata. Serve warm or at room temperature.

apple pie

Classic, old-fashioned apple pie can't be beat. As it bakes, its aroma fills your home with anticipation. With the little bit of extra pastry dough, you could roll out a few leaves to decorate the top of the pie.

MAKES ONE 9-INCH PIE

→ Place the apples in a large bowl and toss with the raisins, maple syrup, lemon juice, cinnamon, and flour. Let this sit for 15 to 30 minutes to macerate.

→ Meanwhile, on a well-floured work surface, roll out one of the chilled dough disks into a 13-inch circle and fit the dough to your pie plate. Roll out the remaining disk into an 11-inch circle for the top crust. Spoon the filling with any juices that have accumulated into the bottom piecrust and dot it with the butter. Cover with the top crust. Trim both the bottom and top crusts, leaving a 1-inch overhang. Tuck the overhang in under the bottom pastry. Flute the edges of the crust as described in the Tips for Pie Dough on page 105. With a knife, make 5 evenly spaced 2-inch slashes in the center of the pie radiating out like the spokes of a wheel. Place the pie in the freezer for about 35 minutes.

→ Preheat the oven to 425 degrees F. Place an oven rack in the lowest position and put a baking stone or sheet pan lined with aluminum foil on the rack.

→ Place the frozen pie directly on the hot stone and bake for 15 minutes. After 15 minutes, reduce the oven temperature to 350 degrees F and bake for an additional 1 hour and 10 minutes. Piecrust will be golden and browned and juices will be oozing. Cool for 2 hours before serving.

7 large tart baking apples, such a Granny Smith, peeled, cored, and sliced

½ cup raisins

¾ cup maple syrup

1½ tablespoons freshly squeezed lemon juice

2 teaspoons ground cinnamon

3 tablespoons einkorn flour

French Pastry Dough (page 102) for a double-crust pie

2 tablespoons cold butter, cut into small pieces

fresh fruit tart

For this recipe I provide two filling choices: A traditional cream cheese filling that very subtly hints of almonds and a dairy- and egg-free variation, consisting mostly of cashews and coconut milk. Both are sweetened with maple syrup. I recommend sliced kiwis, raspberries, and blueberries for the topping because visually they work so well together; however, strawberries, peaches, blackberries, or other fruits would be equally delicious.

MAKES ONE 9-INCH TART

→ Begin by preparing and baking the crust in a 9-inch tart pan.

→ To make the cream cheese filling, beat the cream cheese, maple syrup, vanilla, and almond in a food processor until smooth.

→ Spread the filling into the crust with a spatula. Arrange the kiwi slices overlapping on the outer perimeter of the tart, followed by the blueberries closely placed next to the kiwi in a circular row leaving a center for the remaining raspberries to be placed.

→ In a small heavy saucepan, over low heat, warm the preserves until melted, about 5 minutes. Strain into a small bowl, then brush the strained preserves over the top of the fruit. Serve warm or at room temperature.

Press-In Almond Crust (page 103) for a single-crust pie

CREAM CHEESE FILLING:

1 (8-ounce) package cream cheese

¼ cup maple syrup

½ teaspoon pure vanilla extract

½ teaspoon pure almond extract

TOPPING:

2 large kiwis, peeled, halved lengthwise, and sliced

1 cup (½ pint) fresh blueberries

¾ cups (½ pint) fresh raspberries

¼ cup fruit juice–sweetened apple jelly or apricot preserves

VEGAN VARIATION: CASHEW CREAM FILLING

Substitute this vegan filling for the Cream Cheese Filling.

¼ cup cashews, covered with water and soaked for 2 to 8 hours

½ (13-ounce) can coconut milk

1½ teaspoons pure vanilla extract

1 tablespoon brandy

2 tablespoons water

2 teaspoons agar flakes

2 tablespoons maple syrup

1½ tablespoons coconut oil

→ To make the cashew cream filling, drain the cashews and thoroughly blend in a food processor with the coconut milk, vanilla, and brandy until very creamy and smooth. In a small saucepan, stir together the water, agar flakes, and maple syrup. Bring to a boil, then reduce the heat to low. Cook for 3 minutes, stirring occasionally. Remove the pan from the heat and stir in the coconut oil. Combine the maple syrup mixture and the cashew mixture in a food processor or blender for 30 seconds to combine until creamy.

raspberry pie

This recipe really lets the raspberries take center stage, as there is considerably less sugar than in most raspberry pie recipes. I recommend using the French Pastry Dough for an overall sweeter crust that some palates might find preferable to complement the tart berry filling. The Butter Pastry Dough is also exquisite, while being less sweet.

MAKES ONE 9-INCH PIE

→ In a large bowl, toss the raspberries with the tapioca, arrowroot, lemon juice, and coconut palm sugar. Let sit for 20 to 30 minutes to macerate.

→ Meanwhile, on a well-floured work surface, roll out one of the chilled dough disks into a 13-inch circle and fit the dough to your pie plate. Prick the bottom of the crust with the tines of a fork and place the crust in the freezer for 15 minutes.

→ Preheat the oven to 425 degrees F. Place an oven rack in the lowest position and put a baking stone or sheet pan lined with aluminum foil on the rack.

→ Roll out the remaining disk into an 11-inch circle for the top crust. Brush the chilled bottom crust with the raspberry jam, and pour the filling in. Cover with the top crust. Trim both the bottom and top crusts, leaving a 1-inch overhang. Tuck the overhang in under the bottom pastry. Flute the edges of the crust as described in the Tips for Pie Dough on page 105. With a knife, make 5 evenly spaced 2-inch slashes in the center of the pie radiating out like the spokes of a wheel.

→ Place the pie directly on the baking stone and bake for 30 minutes, then reduce the oven temperature to 350 degrees F. Bake for another 35 minutes or until crust is golden and raspberry filling is oozing. Let the pie cool for about 1½ hours before serving.

5 cups (2½ pints) fresh raspberries

2 tablespoons quick-cooking tapioca

1 tablespoon arrowroot

1 tablespoon freshly squeezed lemon juice

⅔ cup coconut palm sugar

French Pastry Dough (page 102) or Butter Pastry Dough (page 99) for a double-crust pie

3 tablespoons seedless, fruit juice–sweetened raspberry jam

blueberry pie

My grandmother was known to make the best blueberry pie in her family and circle of friends in Cleveland, Ohio. This is saying a lot, because she was a very social woman with a very large family. I believe if my grandma were alive today, she would taste my maple-sweetened blueberry pie and be quite impressed.

MAKES ONE 9-INCH PIE

6 cups (3 pints) fresh blueberries

1 cup maple syrup

⅓ cup quick-cooking tapioca

¼ cup arrowroot

4 teaspoons freshly squeezed lemon juice

½ teaspoon ground cinnamon

Butter Almond Dough (page 100) for a double-crust pie

↠ In a large bowl, toss the blueberries with the maple syrup, tapioca, arrowroot, lemon juice, and cinnamon. Let the berries sit for 20 to 30 minutes to macerate.

↠ Meanwhile, on a well-floured work surface, roll out one of the chilled dough disks into a 13-inch circle and fit the dough to your pie plate. Prick the bottom of the crust with the tines of a fork and place the crust in the freezer for 15 minutes.

↠ Preheat the oven to 425 degrees F. Place an oven rack in the lowest position and put a baking stone or sheet pan lined with aluminum foil on the rack.

↠ Roll out the remaining disk into an 11-inch circle for the top crust. Pour the filling into the chilled bottom crust. Cover with the top crust. Trim both the bottom and top crusts, leaving a 1-inch overhang. Tuck the overhang in under the bottom pastry. Flute the edges of the crust as described in the Tips for Pie Dough on page 105. With a knife, make 5 evenly spaced 2-inch slashes in the center of the pie radiating out like the spokes of a wheel.

↠ Place the pie directly on the baking stone and reduce the oven temperature to 375 degrees F. Bake for 1 hour and 20 minutes or until crust is golden and blueberry filling is oozing. Let the pie cool for about 1½ hours before serving.

peach blueberry pie

Peaches and blueberries are a combination that work marvelously in myriad desserts, and my favorite dessert to house these two celebrated fruits is a pie.

MAKES ONE 9-INCH PIE

→ In a large bowl, combine the peaches and blueberries and toss with the lemon juice, coconut palm sugar, and sea salt. Let this mixture sit for 30 minutes to macerate.

→ Meanwhile, on a well-floured work surface, roll out one of the chilled dough disks into a 13-inch circle and fit the dough to your pie plate. Roll out the remaining disk into an 11-inch circle for the top crust.

→ Preheat the oven to 425 degrees F. Place an oven rack in the lowest position and put a baking stone or sheet pan lined with aluminum foil on the rack.

→ Strain the fruit in a colander placed over a bowl to catch their liquid. In a small saucepan over medium heat, cook ⅔ cup of the liquid until syrupy and reduced by half, about 5 to 7 minutes. Take the pan off the heat and set aside to cool. Place the peaches and blueberries in a medium bowl and toss them with the tapioca and arrowroot.

→ Pour the cooled syrup over the fruit and toss again. Pour the filling into the prepared piecrust. Cover with the top crust. Trim both the bottom and top crusts, leaving a 1-inch overhang. Tuck the overhang in under the bottom pastry. Flute the edges of the crust as described in the Tips for Pie Dough on page 105. With a knife, make 5 evenly spaced 2-inch slashes in the center of the pie radiating out like the spokes of a wheel. Place the pie in the freezer for about 35 minutes.

→ Place the frozen pie directly on the hot stone and bake for 50 minutes until the crust is golden and the peach juices are oozing. Cool for 2½ hours before serving.

1¾ pounds (about 8 medium) fresh peaches, peeled, pitted, and thinly sliced

3 cups (1½ pints) fresh blueberries

1 tablespoon freshly squeezed lemon juice

⅓ cup coconut palm sugar

Pinch of sea salt

French Pastry Dough (page 102) for a double-crust pie

2 teaspoons instant tapioca

2 teaspoons arrowroot

petite peach ginger pies

The inspiration for this dessert came from the talented and acclaimed Flo Braker. The macadamia nuts in the streusel topping harmonize well with the zesty ginger and sweet peaches. If you use frozen peaches, be sure to thaw them for at least an hour before making the filling.

MAKES 8 MUFFIN-SIZE PIES

Butter Pastry Dough (page 99) for a single-crust pie

STREUSEL:

⅓ cup Kamut flour

¼ cup coconut palm sugar

⅓ cup finely chopped unsalted macadamia nuts

¼ teaspoon salt

⅛ teaspoon ground ginger

¼ teaspoon ground cinnamon

¼ cup (½ stick) cold unsalted butter, cut into 4 pieces

FILLING:

1¼ pounds (about 4 medium) ripe fresh or frozen peaches

¼ cup coconut palm sugar

1 tablespoon Kamut flour

½ teaspoon peeled, finely grated fresh ginger

2 teaspoons freshly squeezed lemon juice

→ Preheat the oven to 400 degrees F. Grease and flour 8 standard muffin cups.

→ On a floured surface, roll out the dough to about ⅛-inch thick. Cut out a total of eight 4½-inch-diameter circles with a sharp knife. Using your fingers, gently push the dough into the bottom of the prepared muffin cups.

→ To make the streusel, combine the flour, coconut palm sugar, macadamia nuts, salt, ginger, and cinnamon. Sprinkle the butter pieces over the flour mixture and mix ingredients until the mixture resembles coarse crumbs. Set aside.

→ To make the filling, peel and pit the peaches, and cut them into bite-size pieces, then place them in a large bowl. In a separate bowl, combine the coconut palm sugar and flour. Sprinkle the peaches with ginger and lemon juice, and stir in the dry ingredients. Toss until the peaches are evenly coated with the flour mixture.

→ Divide the filling with its juices evenly among the muffin cups. Sprinkle approximately 1½ tablespoons of streusel over the top of each pie. Bake until the filling bubbles and the pies are golden, about 30 minutes. Let them cool in the pan for 20 minutes before carefully running a thin metal spatula or butter knife around the muffin cups. Cool the pies for an additional 15 minutes in the pan before gently lifting the pies out of their muffin cups or, if needed, inverting them onto a wire rack. Carefully right the pies and serve warm or at room temperature.

pecan honey pie

I make this very rich pie once or twice a year and serve slivers for dessert, though I don't know why I bother—everyone asks for seconds. You might enjoy experimenting with different kinds of honey. If you prefer a mellow, mild taste I recommend using clover honey.

MAKES ONE 9-INCH PIE

Butter Pastry Dough (page 99) for a
   single-crust pie
1 large egg yolk
¼ cup (½ stick) butter, melted
1½ cups honey
1 teaspoon pure vanilla extract
⅓ teaspoon salt
1½ teaspoons orange zest
3 large eggs, lightly beaten
1 heaping cup chopped pecans

→ Preheat the oven to 325 degrees F.

→ On a well-floured work surface, roll the dough out into a 13-inch circle and fit the dough to your pie plate. Trim the edges, leaving a 1-inch overhang. Tuck the overhang under and press against the rim of the pie plate. Flute the crust as described in the Tips for Pie Dough on page 105. Prick the bottom of the crust all over with the tines of a fork. Bake until the edges just begin to brown, about 12 minutes. Remove the crust from the oven. Add a smidgen of water (a few drops) to the egg yolk and mix until it has a smooth and brushable consistency. Brush the crust all over with the egg wash. Return the crust to the oven for another 2 minutes, until the egg wash has set. Place the crust on a rack to cool while preparing the pecan filling. You can leave your oven as you prepare the filling.

→ Combine the butter, honey, vanilla, salt, and orange zest in a medium bowl. Stir in the beaten eggs. Add the pecans and stir to combine. Pour the filling into the prepared crust. Cover the edges of the crust with strips of aluminum foil to prevent them from overbrowning. Bake until set and the pecans smell toasty and carameled, about 35 minutes. Cool completely before serving.

pumpkin pie

My good friend Cassandra, who tested so many of the recipes in this book, made this honey- and maple syrup–sweetened pumpkin pie for her family. Her father is adamant that she serve it at every Thanksgiving henceforth! I couldn't agree more.

MAKES ONE 9-INCH PIE

Butter Almond Dough (page 100) for a single-crust pie
4 large eggs
1 (15-ounce) can cooked pureed pumpkin
½ cup honey
1 tablespoon maple syrup
1 teaspoon pure vanilla extract
½ cup whole milk
½ cup heavy cream
½ teaspoon ground ginger
½ teaspoon ground cinnamon
¼ teaspoon ground nutmeg
1 teaspoon salt

→ Preheat the oven to 375 degrees F. On a well-floured work surface, roll the dough out into a 13-inch circle and fit it to your pie plate. Trim the edges, leaving a 1-inch overhang. Tuck the overhang under and press against the rim of the pie plate. Flute the crust as described in the Tips for Pie Dough on page 105.

→ In a large bowl, beat the eggs until lightly mixed. Add the pumpkin, honey, maple syrup, vanilla, milk, cream, ginger, cinnamon, nutmeg, and salt. Beat until smooth either with a stand mixer or with a whisk. Pour the filling into the crust and then carefully place the pie in the hot oven. The pumpkin filling fills the pie to the brim. Bake until the center is just set and raised, about 45 minutes. The pie will firm up while cooling.

banana cream pie

I particularly love this custard filling, because it is creamy, silky, and caramely. I recommend making the crust the day before, or making the pie on a weekend afternoon and letting it cool until after dinner, as it does take rather long for the filling in this beautiful pie to set. My preference is to fill the shell the day the pie will be enjoyed, so that the crust remains crisp.

MAKES ONE 9-INCH PIE

3 cups whole milk

½ cup maple syrup

⅓ cup coconut palm sugar

⅓ cup light spelt flour or arrowroot, sifted

¼ teaspoon salt

3 large egg yolks

2 tablespoons butter

1 teaspoon pure vanilla extract

3 bananas, sliced

1 prebaked Press-In Almond Crust (page 103) or prebaked Butter Pastry Dough single crust (page 99)

→ Heat the milk and maple syrup in a large saucepan until it reaches 180 degrees F or it is just before boiling. In a medium saucepan, combine the coconut palm sugar, flour, and salt; gradually stir in the scalded milk mixture. Continue to cook over medium heat, stirring constantly, until thickened, about 5 to 7 minutes. Cover the saucepan and stir occasionally for 2 minutes longer to further thicken the mixture.

→ In a small bowl, slightly beat the egg yolks and stir in a small amount, approximately ⅔ cup, of the hot milk mixture until thoroughly combined. Then stir the egg yolk mixture into the milk mixture. Cook for 1 minute longer, stirring constantly. Remove the pan from the heat and stir in the butter and vanilla. Let the filling cool until lukewarm.

→ Place the bananas in the piecrust and pour the filling over the bananas. Let the filling cool completely before serving.

chocolate cream pie

This silky-smooth chocolate pie is unbearably good; the filling, while being rich, is not intense. Though it uses dark chocolate, it tastes almost like milk chocolate. Garnish with dark-chocolate shavings or curls, or strawberries dipped in dark chocolate next to a sprig of mint.

MAKES ONE 9-INCH PIE

✦ Drain the cashews. In a food processor or blender, thoroughly blend the cashews with the coconut milk and vanilla until very creamy and smooth, about 3 to 4 minutes. Set aside.

✦ In a small saucepan, stir together the water, agar flakes, and maple syrup. Bring to a boil and then reduce the heat to a simmer. Cook for 5 minutes, stirring occasionally. Remove the pan from the heat, stir in the coconut oil, and set aside.

✦ Melt the chocolate and Sucanat in a double boiler or a small metal bowl set over a saucepan with a few inches of barely simmering water. (Make sure the bottom of the bowl doesn't touch the water.) Use a rubber spatula to stir the chocolate occasionally and scrape the sides of the bowl so it doesn't burn. When the chocolate has completely melted, remove the pan from the heat. In a food processor, combine the melted chocolate, cashew mixture, and coconut oil mixture until thoroughly combined and milky brown, less than a minute. Pour the filling into the piecrust. Refrigerate until set, about 4 hours.

½ cup raw cashews, covered with water and soaked for 2 to 8 hours

1 (13.5 ounce) can coconut milk

1 tablespoon pure vanilla extract

½ cup water

2 teaspoons agar flakes

¼ cup maple syrup

1 tablespoon coconut oil

3.5 ounces unsweetened chocolate (100% cacao)

¼ cup Sucanat

1 prebaked Press-In Almond Crust (page 103) or prebaked Butter Pastry Dough single crust (page 99)

mixed berry crumble

Crumbles seem to have all the deliciousness of a pie without the labor. This recipe comes together in a snap. Feel free to experiment with whatever berries are in season: Marionberries, strawberries, huckleberries, and raspberries can all be substituted in this very adaptable recipe.

MAKES ONE 9-INCH CRISP

→ Preheat the oven to 350 degrees F. Lightly grease a 9-inch pie plate.

→ To make the filling, in a medium bowl, combine the berries, Sucanat, lemon zest, and flour.

→ To make the topping, in a food processor, pulse the oats, Sucanat, flour, butter, walnuts, and cinnamon until just combined. Pour the berry filling into the prepared pan and sprinkle the topping over the top.

→ Bake until the topping is golden brown and the juice is oozing and bubbling, about 40 minutes.

VEGAN VARIATION: Substitute ½ cup coconut oil for the butter.

FILLING:

4 cups (2 pints) fresh blackberries

2 cups (1 pint) fresh blueberries

2 tablespoons Sucanat

1 teaspoon lemon zest

1 tablespoon light spelt flour

TOPPING:

⅔ cup rolled oats

½ cup Sucanat

¼ cup light spelt flour

½ cup (1 stick) butter

½ cup finely chopped walnuts

2 teaspoons ground cinnamon

nectarine berry buttermilk cobbler

This cobbler has an unsweetened drop-buttermilk-biscuit topping, and the fruit is honey-sweetened. Nectarines and honey are a golden marriage of flavors, and I couldn't resist the opportunity to bring them together in this Southern dessert. This is terrific dessert to make for a summer party. This recipe can also easily be halved; just be sure to adjust the size of your pan to a 9-inch pie pan when doing so.

MAKES ONE 10-BY-14-INCH COBBLER

2½ pounds (about 8 medium) fresh nectarines, peeled, pitted, and sliced

3 tablespoons instant tapioca

⅔ cup honey

1 tablespoon baking powder

2½ cups kamut flour, or 1 cup einkorn flour and 1½ cups kamut flour

6 tablespoons (¾ stick) butter

1½ cups buttermilk

½ cup fresh raspberries

½ cup fresh blackberries

→ Preheat the oven to 400 degrees F. Lightly grease a 10-by-14-inch baking pan.

→ In a large bowl, combine the nectarines, tapioca, and honey, and pour into the prepared pan. Bake while making cobbler dough for 20 minutes to soften the fruit.

→ In a medium bowl, mix the baking powder and flour. With a pastry blender or two knives, cut the butter into the flour mixture until it resembles coarse, pea-size crumbs. Stir in the buttermilk with a fork, making a cobbler dough that just begins to hold together, but not completely. Set aside.

→ Remove the nectarines from the oven and fold the raspberries and blackberries into the hot nectarines. Return the pan to the oven for 5 minutes to heat, until the berries are heated through. Then remove the pan from the oven and quickly drop spoonfuls of cobbler topping to cover the fruit.

→ Increase the oven temperature to 425 degrees F and bake until topping is golden brown and the juice is oozing and bubbling, about 20 minutes.

strawberry and macadamia nut crisp

This crisp topping includes shredded coconut and macadamia nuts, offering a Hawaiian taste, if you will. The strawberries are sweetened with coconut palm sugar and dressed with just a little bit of lemon juice and a smidgen of orange zest. I enjoy this crisp warm or chilled, with a dollop of creamy yogurt.

MAKES ONE 9-INCH CRISP

→ Preheat the oven to 375 degrees F. Lightly grease a 9-inch square baking dish.

→ To make the filling, in a large bowl, mix together the strawberries, coconut palm sugar, tapioca, lemon juice, and orange zest. Pour into the prepared baking dish.

→ To make the topping, in a separate medium bowl, stir together the flour, coconut, coconut palm sugar, macadamia nuts, baking powder, and salt. Use your fingers to mix the butter into the dry ingredients until the mixture looks like coarse meal.

→ Sprinkle the topping over the filling. Bake until the topping is golden brown and crispy, and the filling is bubbling, 35 to 40 minutes. Let cool for 1 hour before serving.

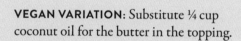

VEGAN VARIATION: Substitute ¼ cup coconut oil for the butter in the topping.

FILLING:

4 cups (2 pints) fresh strawberries, halved

¼ cup plus 1 tablespoon coconut palm sugar

2 tablespoons instant tapioca

1 tablespoon freshly squeezed lemon juice

½ teaspoon orange zest

TOPPING:

½ cup barley flour, or ¼ cup einkorn flour and ¼ cup barley flour

½ cup shredded coconut

¼ cup coconut palm sugar

⅓ cup chopped macadamia nuts

¼ teaspoon baking powder

Pinch of salt

¼ cup (½ stick) cold unsalted butter, chopped into cubes

cakes & frostings

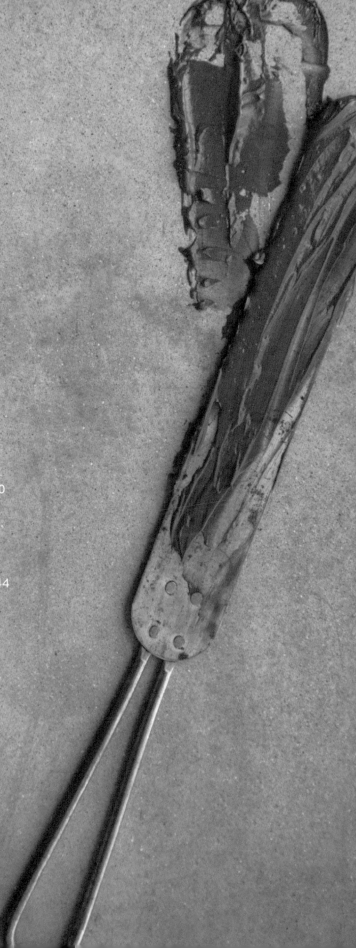

CAKE CONJURES UP DEAR memories of being with my dad at Flying Apron Bakery in its early days. Working almost around the clock, we would even have cake for breakfast. In those days we frosted at minimum a half-dozen special-order cakes a day, and often almost a hundred cupcakes as well. My mom is also a very talented baker. Most often she would bake one of two cakes: The first was a moist yellow cake with fluffy white frosting drizzled with unsweetened chocolate. The second, my dad's absolute favorite, was a lemon poppyseed cake, which I offer as a variation of the Yellow Cake (page 134).

In this chapter you will find celebration cakes with creamy frostings, and sophisticated cakes with no frostings at all. The stronger-flavored cakes, such as the Rich Chocolate Torte (page 127), Olive Oil Cake (page 137), Gingerbread Cake (page 139), and Buckwheat Breton Cake (page 140), are probably more suited for adult palates. The rest would greatly please young and old alike.

rich chocolate torte (GF)

Rozanne Gold, a very talented chef and author, really deserves the credit for this recipe. I did very little to alter this decadent chocolate torte. Serve this very simple and fancy dessert with fresh berries, perhaps after a romantic dinner.

MAKES ONE 9-INCH TORTE

→ Preheat the oven to 375 degrees F. Line the bottom of a 9-inch springform pan with parchment paper and grease the sides of the pan with about ½ tablespoon of butter.

→ In a large bowl using an electric mixer, or in the bowl of a stand mixer fitted with the paddle attachment, beat the eggs with a pinch of salt on high speed until tripled in volume. This will take about 8 to 10 minutes.

→ Melt the butter and chocolate in a double boiler or a small metal bowl set over a saucepan with a few inches of barely simmering water. (Make sure the bottom of the bowl doesn't touch the water.) Use a rubber spatula to stir occasionally and scrape the sides of the bowl so the chocolate doesn't burn. When the butter and chocolate have completely melted, fold the chocolate mixture into the eggs. Stir in the vanilla. Pour the batter into the prepared pan. Bake for 18 minutes, or until set around the edges. The center of the cake will be oozy and very soft.

5 extra-large eggs

½ cup (1 stick) plus 2 tablespoons unsalted butter, plus more for greasing the pan

1 pound Maple-Sweetened Chocolate (page 46), chopped

1 teaspoon pure vanilla extract

triple-layer chocolate
sour cream cake

This divinely moist cake is luscious, rich, and just the thing for a special occasion or family gathering. My favorite way to serve it is frosted with Chocolate Cream Cheese Frosting (page 117).

MAKES ONE 9-INCH, THREE-LAYER CAKE

2 cups barley flour, or 1¼ cups einkorn flour and ¾ cup barley flour, sifted

⅔ cup cocoa powder

1 teaspoon salt

1 teaspoon baking soda

½ cup (1 stick) butter

3 large eggs

1 cup maple syrup

1 teaspoon pure vanilla extract

¾ cup sour cream

¼ cup whole milk

→ Preheat the oven to 350 degrees F. Grease three 9-inch cake pans and line them with circles of cut-out greased parchment paper.

→ In a medium bowl, sift together the flour, cocoa powder, salt, and baking soda. In a large bowl using an electric mixer, or in the bowl of a stand mixer fitted with the paddle attachment, cream the butter until light and fluffy. Beat in the eggs, one at a time, followed by the maple syrup and vanilla. Add the dry ingredients in 3 parts, alternating with the sour cream and milk, mixing only until just combined. Pour the batter into the prepared pans and spread it evenly with a spatula. Bake for 25 to 30 minutes, or until a wooden toothpick inserted into the center of the cake comes out with just a few very moist crumbs attached—this is a moist cake, so be careful not to overbake. Remove the pans to wire racks to cool for 20 minutes. Turn the cakes out of the pans, peeling off the parchment paper, and place them on the racks to continue cooling for 3 hours before frosting.

→ Once the cakes have cooled, place one layer on a cake platter and spread your frosting of choice on top, leaving a 1-inch border. Repeat with the remaining layers.

Tips on Making Cakes

→ Always have your butter and eggs at room temperature.

→ Shiny metal pans bake cakes the most evenly.

→ Be sure to grease your cake pans and lightly dust them with flour.

→ Bake your cakes positioned in the very middle of your oven on the center rack.

→ To allow for variations in oven temperature, check your cakes for doneness about 4 minutes before the recipes call for. Your cake is done when a wooden toothpick inserted in the center comes out clean or with a few crumbs attached to it. If it comes out wet, bake the cake for another 2 to 3 minutes, then test again. Continue testing every 2 to 3 minutes, as it is easy to overbake.

red velvet chocolate beet cake

I adapted this recipe from Laura Martin's Green Market Baking Book. *I love the way the grated beets add moisture and contribute their vibrant magenta color. My favorite topping for this cake is the Maple Whipped Cream (page 148), though the frostings in this chapter are delicious too. I like to decorate this cake with fresh mint and drizzled either melted Maple-Sweetened Chocolate (page 46) or shavings of bittersweet chocolate, and serve it alongside fresh cherries or blackberries.*

MAKES ONE 9-INCH, THREE-LAYER CAKE

→ Preheat the oven to 350 degrees F. Lightly grease three 9-inch cake pans with butter and dust them lightly with cocoa powder.

→ Place the beets in a colander to drain excess moisture while you prepare the rest of the ingredients. In a large bowl, whisk the oil, maple syrup, and honey until well blended.

→ Add the eggs, one at a time, beating until smooth after each addition. Mix in the vanilla and almond.

→ Sift together the flour, cocoa, baking soda, and salt. Gently fold the flour mixture into the wet ingredients, followed by the beets. Pour the batter into the prepared pans and spread it evenly with a spatula.

→ Bake until a wooden toothpick inserted into the center of the cakes comes out clean, 20 to 25 minutes. Remove the pans to wire racks to cool for 20 minutes. Turn the cakes out of the pans onto the racks to continue cooling for 3 hours before frosting.

→ In a small bowl, combine the maple syrup and kirsch. Once the cakes have cooled, place one layer on a cake platter, brush it with the syrup mixture, and spread your frosting of choice on top, leaving a 1-inch border. Repeat with the remaining layers.

3 medium red beets, cooked, cooled, and finely grated to measure 2 cups

1 cup light olive oil or canola oil

¾ cup pure maple syrup

½ cup honey

3 large eggs

1 teaspoon pure vanilla extract

1 teaspoon pure almond extract

2 cups Kamut flour, or 1 cup einkorn flour and 1 cup Kamut flour, sifted

¾ cup cocoa powder

2 teaspoons baking soda

½ teaspoon sea salt

¼ cup maple syrup

2 tablespoons kirsch

honey spice cake (GF)

This cake is really fabulous for dessert, afternoon tea, or even as a brunch coffee cake. Using all teff flour gives it a bread-like texture, while the version made with half tapioca flour is more like an angel food cake. My favorite way to enjoy it is with cardamom-infused coffee: grind your coffee beans with a few cloves of cardamom and brew as usual. It is even more tasty with a bit of honey and milk. If you decide to make this cake into the three-layer version, I recommend frosting with the Cream Cheese Honey Frosting (page 147).

MAKES ONE BUNDT CAKE OR ONE 8-INCH, THREE-LAYER CAKE

½ cup (1 stick) butter

¾ cup honey, plus more for drizzling the cake

2 cups teff flour, or 1 cup tapioca flour and 1 cup teff flour

2 teaspoons baking powder

½ teaspoon salt

1 teaspoon ground cinnamon

½ teaspoon ground cloves

¼ teaspoon ground nutmeg

2 large eggs, separated

½ cup whole milk

½ cup chopped nuts

½ cup chopped raisins (optional)

To make a **FIVE-LAYER CAKE**, double the recipe and divide the batter between five 8-inch cake pans.

→ Preheat the oven to 350 degrees F. Grease and flour a tube cake pan or three 8-inch cake pans.

→ In a large bowl using an electric mixer, or in the bowl of a stand mixer fitted with the paddle attachment, cream the butter and honey together thoroughly. In a separate large bowl, sift the flour, baking powder, salt, cinnamon, cloves, and nutmeg together. Add 1 cup of the dry ingredients to the wet mixture and mix well. Add the egg yolks and mix. Add the remaining dry ingredients alternately with the milk in 3 additions. Fold in the nuts and raisins. Beat the egg whites until stiff and fold them in. Pour the batter into the prepared cake pans. Bake until a wooden toothpick inserted into the center of the tube cake comes out clean, about 1 hour. When baking in 8-inch cake pans, check the cakes after 35 minutes for doneness.

→ While the cake is still hot, drizzle honey over it. If using the Bundt pan, let the cake cool in the pan for 30 minutes before turning it out. If using the cake pans, let the cake cool in the pans for 10 minutes before removing the cakes to wire racks to continue cooling. Let the cake cool completely before frosting, at least 1 hour.

yellow cake

When I was growing up, my mother often kept yellow cake rounds already baked and wrapped in the freezer. Every once in a while after school, my sister and I would get our hands on one of these frozen cakes and go to town! This is a wholesome version of that yellow cake. My two favorite frostings for this cake are Dark Chocolate Frosting (page 145) and Cream Cheese Honey Frosting (page 147). If you feel like experimenting, add some jam or berries to the layers with the cream cheese frosting.

MAKES ONE 9-INCH, THREE-LAYER CAKE OR ONE 13-BY-9-INCH CAKE

2¼ cups light spelt flour, or 1 cup light spelt flour and 1¼ cups einkorn flour

2½ teaspoons baking powder

½ teaspoon salt

½ cup (1 stick) butter, at room temperature

¾ cup maple syrup

3 large eggs

1½ teaspoons pure vanilla extract

1¼ cups whole milk

VARIATION: To make this a lemon poppy seed cake, add 2 tablespoons of poppy seeds and the juice of one lemon to the batter.

→ Preheat the oven to 375 degrees F. Grease three 9-inch cake pans or one 13-by-9-inch baking pan and lightly flour.

→ In a medium bowl, sift together the flour, baking powder, and salt. In a large bowl using an electric mixer, or in the bowl of a stand mixer fitted with the paddle attachment, beat the butter on medium to high speed until creamy. Gradually add the maple syrup on medium speed until well combined, scraping the bowl every so often. Add the eggs and vanilla. Add the dry ingredients alternately with the milk in 2 additions. After all ingredients are incorporated, continue beating on low speed for about 2 minutes. Pour the batter into the prepared pans and spread it evenly with a spatula. Bake until a wooden toothpick inserted into the center of the cake comes out clean, about 30 minutes. Remove the pans to wire racks to cool for 10 minutes. Turn the cakes out of the pans onto the racks to continue cooling for 3 hours before frosting.

→ For the three-layer cake, once the cakes have cooled, place one layer on a cake platter and spread your frosting of choice on top, leaving a 1-inch border. Repeat with the remaining layers.

vanilla cake

Whenever I have this cake, I recall friends' and family's wedding celebrations I have enjoyed over the years. It is lovely with Maple Whipped Cream (page 148) and thinly sliced strawberries or raspberries between the layers.

MAKES ONE 9-INCH, THREE-LAYER CAKE

→ Preheat the oven to 325 degrees F. Grease three 9-inch cake pans and line them with circles of cut-out greased and floured parchment paper.

→ In a large bowl using an electric mixer, or in the bowl of a stand mixer fitted with the paddle attachment, beat the egg whites and honey on medium speed until foamy. Add the melted butter and continue to beat for 3 minutes. In a medium bowl, sift together the flours, salt, and baking powder. Gradually add the dry ingredients and mix on the lowest speed. When they are moistened, turn the mixer back up to medium speed and continue to beat, adding the water and vanilla. The batter will be thin and creamy. Pour the batter into the prepared pans. Bake for 20 to 25 minutes or until a wooden toothpick inserted into the center of the cake comes out clean. Remove the pans to wire racks to cool for 10 minutes. Turn the cakes out of the pans onto the racks to continue cooling for 3 hours before frosting.

→ Once the cakes have cooled, place one layer on a cake platter and spread your frosting of choice on top, leaving a 1-inch border. Repeat with the remaining layers.

6 large egg whites

1 cup honey

6 tablespoons (¾ stick) butter, melted

1 cup Kamut flour, or ½ cup einkorn flour and ½ cup Kamut flour, sifted

1 cup einkorn flour

¼ teaspoon salt

2 teaspoons baking powder

½ cup water

1 tablespoon plus 1 teaspoon pure vanilla extract

carrot cake

Moist carrot cake abundant with raisins, walnuts, toasted coconut, and spices is a party favorite. The freshly grated nutmeg is worth the little bit of extra effort. I like to ice this cake with either traditional Cream Cheese Honey Frosting (page 147) or Vanilla Maple Frosting (page 148).

MAKES ONE 13-BY-9-INCH CAKE

1¾ cups finely grated carrots

½ cup raisins

½ cup chopped walnuts

⅓ cup freshly squeezed orange juice

1 tablespoon pure vanilla extract

½ cup (1 stick) butter, at room temperature

1 cup maple syrup

2 large eggs

2 cups light spelt flour, or 1 cup einkorn flour and 1 cup light spelt flour

½ cup toasted shredded coconut

2 teaspoons baking powder

1 teaspoon baking soda

1½ teaspoons ground cinnamon

½ teaspoon ground ginger

¼ teaspoon freshly grated nutmeg

½ teaspoon salt

→ Preheat the oven to 350 degrees F. Grease and flour a 13-by-9-inch baking pan.

→ In a medium bowl, combine the carrots with the raisins, walnuts, orange juice, and vanilla. In a large bowl using an electric mixer, or in the bowl of a stand mixer fitted with the paddle attachment, cream the butter and maple syrup until light and fluffy. Add the eggs one at a time, beating well after each addition. In a separate medium bowl, whisk the flour, coconut, baking powder, baking soda, cinnamon, ginger, nutmeg, and salt. Add the dry ingredients to the butter mixture alternately with the carrot mixture in 2 additions, mixing until just combined. Spoon the batter into the prepared baking pan and bake for 40 minutes, or until a wooden toothpick inserted into the center of the cake comes out clean. Cool the cake in the pan for 10 minutes, then slice and serve warm. If you plan to frost the cake, let it cool completely.

olive oil cake

This lovely cake is light and moist, and the rosemary with honey and citrus awakens your palate. I've served it at brunch, with afternoon espresso and tea, and for a summer dessert with fresh peaches.

MAKES 1 BUNDT CAKE

→ Preheat the oven to 325 degrees F. Grease and flour an 11-cup Bundt pan.

→ In a large bowl using an electric mixer, or in the bowl of a stand mixer fitted with the paddle attachment, beat the eggs and honey in a large mixing bowl until pale yellow on medium-high speed, about 1 minute. Add the flour, lemon zest, rosemary, oil, milk, and Grand Marnier and stir with a wooden spoon until well combined. Add the baking powder and stir until combined. Scrape the batter into the prepared pan, and smooth the top with the back of the spoon. Bake until the cake is a deep golden brown and a wooden toothpick inserted into the center of the cake comes out clean, about 45 minutes. Remove the pan to a wire rack to cool completely. After the cake has cooled, turn it out onto a serving plate.

2 large eggs

1 cup honey

3 cups light spelt flour, or 1½ cups einkorn flour and 1½ cups light spelt flour

¼ teaspoon lemon zest

1½ teaspoons dried chopped rosemary

¾ cup extra-virgin olive oil

⅔ cup whole milk

3 tablespoons Grand Marnier or other citrus-flavored liqueur

1 tablespoon baking powder

gingerbread cake

This bold gingerbread is abundant with blackstrap molasses, lots of fresh and ground ginger, and even a bit of black pepper. Make this cake even more tasty by soaking the raisins in brandy overnight to plump them. Serve it with a dollop of whipped cream to complement its full-bodied flavor.

MAKES ONE 13-BY-9-INCH CAKE

→ Preheat the oven to 350 degrees F. Lightly grease and flour a 13-by-9-inch baking pan. Strain the raisins and set them aside.

→ In a medium bowl, combine the flours, cocoa, cinnamon, ginger, baking soda, baking powder, salt, cloves, and pepper. In a small bowl, stir together the molasses, maple syrup, water, and oil. Stir in the fresh ginger. In a large bowl using an electric mixer, or in the bowl of a stand mixer fitted with the paddle attachment, beat the butter on medium speed until creamy. Add the eggs one at a time, mixing well after each addition. Add the dry ingredients to the butter alternately with the molasses mixture in 3 additions, mixing until just combined. Fold in the raisins and orange zest. Pour the batter into the prepared pan. Bake until a wooden toothpick inserted into the center of the cake comes out with a few crumbs, about 45 minutes. Let the cake cool for about 1 hour before serving.

> To make 6 miniature gingerbread cakes, lightly grease and flour 6 **MINI BUNDT** pans. Distribute the batter equally between them and bake for 17 minutes.

- ¾ cup raisins, soaked in hot water for about 30 minutes
- 1¾ cups barley flour
- ⅔ cup buckwheat flour or ⅔ cup einkorn flour
- 1 tablespoon cocoa powder
- 2 teaspoons ground cinnamon
- 2 teaspoons ground ginger
- 1½ teaspoons baking soda
- ½ teaspoon baking powder
- ½ teaspoon salt
- ½ teaspoon ground cloves
- ¼ teaspoon freshly ground black pepper
- 1 cup blackstrap molasses
- ¾ cup maple syrup
- ½ cup water
- ¼ cup canola oil
- 2 tablespoons peeled, grated fresh ginger
- ½ cup (1 stick) butter
- 2 large eggs
- 1 teaspoon finely grated orange zest

buckwheat breton cake (GF)

Breton cake is a traditional butter cake, almost a shortbread, that has been enjoyed in Brittany, France, since the late 1800s. Because buckwheat grows so well in Brittany and is a part of that region's cuisine, I felt that creating a Breton cake with buckwheat flour would be appropriate. I later learned that Breton buckwheat cake has been a tradition of Brittany for some time.

MAKES ONE 8-INCH CAKE

1 cup (2 sticks) butter, at room temperature

1 cup Sucanat or coconut palm sugar

4 large egg yolks

1 tablespoon Armagnac

1½ cups buckwheat flour, or ¾ cup tapioca flour and ¾ cup buckwheat flour

½ teaspoon salt

¾ cup finely chopped walnuts

⇢ Preheat the oven to 350 degrees F. Grease and flour an 8-inch round cake pan. Set ingredients out on counter to come to room temperature.

⇢ In a large bowl using an electric mixer, or in the bowl of a stand mixer fitted with the paddle attachment, beat the butter and coconut palm sugar for about 3 minutes. With the mixer on medium speed, add the egg yolks one at a time, beating well after each addition. Stir in the Armagnac. Gradually add the flour and salt, then fold in the walnuts. Bake for 45 minutes, or until a wooden toothpick inserted into the center of the cake comes out with a few moist crumbs attached. Note that this is a moist cake; be careful not to overbake.

coconut cloud cake

This moist cake is abundant with coconut milk. Ice it with Vanilla Maple Frosting (page 148) and decorate with toasted coconut for a triple tropical treat. Serve it alongside a glass of refreshing iced green tea. Note: If you won't be serving it right away, keep it refrigerated. Be sure to cover and store leftovers in the refrigerator.

MAKES ONE 9-INCH, DOUBLE-LAYER CAKE

→ Preheat the oven to 375 degrees F. Grease and lightly flour two 9-inch round cake pans.

→ To make the cake, in a medium bowl, sift together the flour, baking powder, and salt. In a large bowl using an electric mixer, or in the bowl of a stand mixer fitted with the paddle attachment, beat the butter on medium to high speed until creamy. Gradually add the maple syrup, beating on medium speed until well combined, scraping the bowl every so often. Beat in the eggs, vanilla, and almond extract. Add the dry ingredients alternately with the coconut milk in 2 additions. Continue beating on low speed until your batter reaches the ribbon stage, about 2 minutes. Fold in the shredded coconut. Spoon the batter into the prepared pans. Bake until a wooden toothpick inserted into the center of the cake comes out clean, 20 to 25 minutes. Cool the cake in the pans for 10 minutes. Remove the pans to wire racks to cool for 10 minutes. Turn the cakes out of the pans onto the racks to continue cooling for 3 hours before frosting.

→ To make the filling, in a medium bowl, thoroughly combine all the ingredients. Using the wrong end of a wooden spoon, poke holes about 2 inches apart in one of the cakes, covering the entire surface. Spread ½ of the filling on the cake. Repeat with the second layer. Frost and decorate the top and sides with the frosting and the coconut.

CAKE:

2½ cups light spelt flour, or 1 cup einkorn flour and 1½ cups light spelt flour

2½ teaspoons baking powder

½ teaspoon salt

½ cup (1 stick) butter, at room temperature

¾ cup maple syrup

3 large eggs

1½ teaspoons pure vanilla extract

1 teaspoon pure almond extract

1¼ cups coconut milk

½ cup unsweetened shredded coconut

FILLING:

¼ cup maple syrup

½ cup sour cream

2 tablespoons whole milk

¼ cup unsweetened flaked coconut

½ teaspoon pure almond extract

Vanilla Maple Frosting (page 148)
½ cup toasted large-flaked coconut

carrot pineapple cupcakes

These cupcakes are made with juicy, sweet pineapple and crunchy, buttery macadamia nuts, giving them a slightly tropical twist. I recommend frosting these with Vanilla Maple Frosting (page 148); note that you'll need to halve the frosting recipe (or double the cupcakes).

MAKES 10 CUPCAKES

1½ cups grated carrots

½ cup chopped macadamia nuts

1 cup chopped fresh or canned pineapple

1¾ cups light spelt flour, or 1 cup light spelt flour and ¾ cup einkorn flour

1 teaspoon baking powder

¾ teaspoon baking soda

¾ teaspoon ground ginger

½ teaspoon ground cinnamon

½ teaspoon ground cloves

½ teaspoon salt

⅔ cup coconut palm sugar

2 teaspoons pure vanilla extract

⅓ cup light olive oil

2 large eggs

→ Preheat the oven to 350 degrees F. Line 10 cupcake cups with foil or paper liners.

→ In a medium bowl, combine the carrots, nuts, and pineapple. In a separate medium bowl, whisk together the flour, baking powder, baking soda, ginger, cinnamon, cloves, and salt. In a large bowl using an electric mixer, or in the bowl of a stand mixer fitted with the paddle attachment, beat the coconut palm sugar, vanilla, and oil on medium speed. Add eggs one at a time, beating well after each addition. Add the dry ingredients alternately with the carrot mixture in 2 additions, mixing until just combined.

→ Spoon the batter into the prepared cups and bake until a wooden toothpick inserted into the center of the cake comes out clean, about 17 minutes. Remove to a wire rack to cool completely before frosting.

cherry almond coffee cake

This honey-sweetened cinnamon cake full of cherries and topped with an oat-y almond streusel is almost unfairly tasty. If I am going to splurge at breakfast, I'll order a piece of coffee cake from time to time, hoping it will be as scrumptious as this wholesome version. So far nothing compares.

MAKES ONE 8-INCH SQUARE CAKE

1 cup teff flour

1 cup light spelt flour

1 teaspoon baking powder

1 teaspoon baking soda

½ teaspoon salt

1 teaspoon ground cinnamon

1 cup chopped frozen cherries

½ cup canola oil

2 large eggs

⅓ cup honey

1 cup plain whole-milk yogurt (my
    favorite is goat's milk, but all kinds
    work well)

1 teaspoon pure almond extract

STREUSEL TOPPING:

¼ cup rolled oats

¼ cup teff flour

⅓ cup slivered almonds

3 tablespoons cold butter, chopped

3 tablespoons Sucanat

¼ tablespoon ground cinnamon

Pinch of salt

1 tablespoon maple syrup

→ Preheat the oven to 375 degrees F. Lightly grease and flour an 8-inch square pan.

→ In a large bowl, combine the flours, baking powder, baking soda, salt, and cinnamon. Add the cherries and toss to coat. In a medium bowl, whisk the oil, eggs, honey, yogurt, and almond extract. Fold the yogurt mixture into the dry ingredients until just blended.

→ To make the streusel topping, in a small bowl, combine the oats, flour, almonds, butter, Sucanat, cinnamon, and salt. Rub the ingredients together with your fingers until the butter is distributed and it resembles coarse meal. Stir in the maple syrup.

→ Spoon the batter into the prepared pan and sprinkle the streusel topping on top. Bake until the cake is golden and a wooden toothpick inserted into the center of the cake comes out clean, 30 to 35 minutes. Serve warm or at room temperature.

 GLUTEN-FREE VARIATION: Substitute 1 cup tapioca flour for the light spelt flour.

dark chocolate frosting

Being a chocolate lover, this is the frosting for me. It is very temperamental, being most spreadable when it is not too cold and not too warm. When I make the frosting ahead of time, I store it in an airtight container, rewarm it slightly in a bowl set over a pot full of simmering water, and rewhip it before using.

MAKES ABOUT 3 CUPS FROSTING

→ Melt the chocolate in a double boiler or a small metal bowl set over a saucepan with a few inches of barely simmering water. (Make sure the bottom of the bowl doesn't touch the water.) Use a rubber spatula to stir the chocolate occasionally and scrape the sides of the bowl so the chocolate doesn't burn. When the chocolate has completely melted, remove the pan from the heat and set it aside.

→ Meanwhile, in a large bowl using an electric mixer, or in the bowl of a stand mixer fitted with the paddle attachment, on high speed, beat the maple syrup, butter, vanilla, salt, and espresso. Once the chocolate has melted, gradually beat it into the butter mixture. Continue to beat for 5 minutes, scraping down the sides of the bowl every so often. Cover the frosting and chill it in the refrigerator for about 30 minutes. Whip it again until smooth before using.

1 pound unsweetened chocolate, chopped

¾ cup maple syrup

1 cup (2 sticks) unsalted butter

1 tablespoon pure vanilla extract

¼ teaspoon salt

1 tablespoon finely ground espresso (optional)

chocolate cream cheese frosting

This frosting comes together rapidly and is easy to work with. It reminds me of chocolate cheese cake. The flavor is milder than the Dark Chocolate Frosting (page 145), making it a good choice for the little ones.

MAKES ABOUT 3 CUPS FROSTING

⇢ In a large bowl using an electric mixer, or in the bowl of a stand mixer fitted with the paddle attachment, beat all the ingredients on high speed until light and fluffy. Cover the frosting and chill it in the refrigerator until it is stiff enough to spread, about 30 minutes.

2 (8-ounce) packages cream cheese
½ cup maple syrup
½ cup sifted cocoa powder
2 teaspoons pure vanilla extract
Pinch of salt

cream cheese honey frosting

I use this recipe for cakes as well as frosting cookies. It is an ideal frosting to add color to; natural food coloring made from beets, turmeric, blueberry juice, and the like can be found at health-food stores.

MAKES ABOUT 2½ CUPS FROSTING

⇢ In a large bowl using an electric mixer, or in the bowl of a stand mixer fitted with the paddle attachment, beat the cream cheese, honey, vanilla, salt, and lemon zest on high speed until light and fluffy. Cover the frosting and chill it in the refrigerator until it is stiff enough to spread, about 30 minutes.

2 (8-ounce) packages cream cheese
⅓ cup honey
2 teaspoons pure vanilla extract
Pinch of salt
1 teaspoon lemon zest

vanilla maple frosting

The addition of whipped cream gives this maple-sweetened frosting a smooth, light consistency. This frosting spreads with ease and has a beautiful, clean look.

MAKES ABOUT 4 CUPS FROSTING

1½ cups cold heavy cream

2 (8-ounce) packages cream cheese

½ cup maple syrup

1 tablespoon pure vanilla extract

→ In a medium bowl using an electric mixer or a whisk, whip the cream until stiff. In a large bowl using an electric mixer, or in the bowl of a stand mixer fitted with the paddle attachment, whip the cream cheese until smooth, and then blend in the maple syrup and vanilla. Fold the whipped cream into the cream cheese mixture using a spatula.

maple whipped cream

This simple topping can be enjoyed on a great variety of cakes. It goes particularly well with the Red Velvet Chocolate Beet Cake (page 131), Honey Spice Cake (page 132), and Gingerbread Cake (page 139).

MAKES 5½ CUPS WHIPPED CREAM

3 cups cold heavy cream

3 tablespoons maple syrup

→ In a large bowl using an electric mixer or a whisk, whip the cream and maple syrup until soft peaks hold.

acknowledgments

THANK YOU Joseph, your strength and love is unequivocal. Thank you Lilli, you are my ultimate inspiration. Thank you Mom, Dad, Kat, Malcolm, Jer, Leon, Jules, Andy, Rosie, Josh, Sherry, and Caleb. All of your love and support is deeply felt. Thank you Tami Hafzalla for being a teacher and a friend. Thank you Gabrielle Anderson for our long walks and friendship. Thank you Cassandra Parker for your thorough research and ever so insightful writing about the ingredients. Thank you to the amazing community of friends, new and old, who tested this collection of recipes. I am overwhelmed with gratitude and a feeling of true support by your willingness to dive into baking and give such detailed feedback. Thank you to the entire Sasquatch Books team! Working with all of you is such a creative, productive, and joyful experience. Thank you Susan Roxborough for your steady strength, grace, and positive energy. This book really happened because of you. Thank you Michelle Hope Anderson for your efficacious, cheerful, and instructive communication. Thank you Charity Burggraaf, your photography evokes mouthwatering confidence and clarity, and makes the book visually standout. Thank you Julie Hopper, your finesse with food and visual insight is that of a true artist. Thank you Anna Goldstein for your design brilliance, making the book so contemporary in its approachability and so classically beautiful at the same time. Thank you to the loving community I live in that surrounds me with meaningful and joyful connections.

Finding Alternative
flours & sweeteners

einkorn flour

ONLINE AT: Amazon.com
IN STORE AT: PCC Natural Markets
(in the greater Seattle area) and other
local food co-ops

barley flour

ONLINE AT: Amazon.com and
ShopOrganic.com
IN STORE AT: most grocery stores
(Bob's Red Mill is a common brand), or
Whole Foods and other local food co-ops
(in the bulk section)

buckwheat flour

ONLINE AT: Amazon.com and
ShopOrganic.com
IN STORE AT: most grocery stores
(Bob's Red Mill is a common brand)

spelt flour

ONLINE AT: ShopOrganic.com,
Nuts.com, and Amazon.com
IN STORE AT: most grocery stores
(in the baking or bulk food section)

kamut flour

ONLINE AT: Amazon.com or Nuts.com
IN STORE AT: most grocery stores
(Bob's Red Mill is a common brand)
and most food co-ops

teff flour

ONLINE AT: Amazon.com,
ShopOrganic.com, and Nuts.com
IN STORE AT: many grocery stores
(in the baking section)

tapioca

ONLINE AT: Amazon.com and
ShopOrganic.com
IN STORE AT: most grocery stores
NOTE: Tapioca flour and tapioca starch
are the same

coconut palm sugar

ONLINE AT: Amazon.com and Nuts.com
IN STORE AT: many specialty food stores
and most food co-ops

sucanat

ONLINE AT: Amazon.com and Nuts.com
IN STORE AT: many specialty food stores
and most food co-ops

index

conversions

volume

UNITED STATES	METRIC	IMPERIAL
¼ teaspoon	1.25 milliliters	
½ teaspoon	2.5 milliliters	
1 teaspoon	5 milliliters	
½ tablespoon	7.5 milliliters	
1 tablespoon	15 milliliters	
⅛ cup	30 milliliters	1 fluid ounces
¼ cup	60 milliliters	2 fluid ounces
⅓ cup	80 milliliters	2.5 fluid ounces
½ cup	125 milliliters	4 fluid ounces
1 cup	250 milliliters	8 fluid ounces
2 cups (1 pint)	500 milliliters	16 fluid ounces
1 quart	1 liter	32 fluid ounces

length

UNITED STATES	METRIC
⅛ inch	3 millimeters
¼ inch	6 millimeters
½ inch	1.25 centimeters
1 inch	2.5 centimeters
1 foot	30 centimeters

weight

AVOIRDUPOIS	METRIC
¼ ounce	7 grams
½ ounce	15 grams
1 ounce	30 grams
2 ounces	60 grams
3 ounces	90 grams
4 ounces	115 grams
5 ounces	150 grams
6 ounces	175 grams
7 ounces	200 grams
8 ounces (½ pound)	225 grams
9 ounces	250 grams
10 ounces	300 grams

AVOIRDUPOIS	METRIC
11 ounces	325 grams
12 ounces	350 grams
13 ounces	375 grams
14 ounces	400 grams
15 ounces	425 grams
16 ounces (1 pound)	450 grams
1½ pounds	750 grams
2 pounds	900 grams
2¼ pounds	1 kilogram
3 pounds	1.4 kilograms
4 pounds	1.8 kilograms

temperature

OVEN MARK	FARENHEIT	CELSIUS	GAS
Very cool	250–275	130–140	½–1
Cool	300	150	2
Warm	325	165	3
Moderate	350	175	4
Moderately hot	375	190	5
	400	200	6
Hot	425	220	7
	450	230	8
Very Hot	475	245	9

About the *author*

JENNIFER KATZINGER and her father first opened the doors of the Flying Apron Bakery in 2002, recognizing the value in organic baked goods made with unrefined flours and sweeteners. After growing the bakery from a tiny take-out window in Seattle's University District to a spacious, lovely cafe in the city's Fremont neighborhood, Jennifer sold the bakery in 2010, and it continues to thrive.

After selling the bakery, Jennifer pursued her two greatest passions—being a mother and continuing to develop delicious, healthy recipes. She is delighted to bring you her fifth cookbook, a wonderful collection of recipes made with wholesome ancient grain flours and alternative sweeteners.

Jennifer earned a BA in English Literature from the University of Washington and pursued a Masters in Industrial Design from the Pratt Institute in Brooklyn, New York. She lives in Seattle with her husband, Joseph, their daughter, Lillian, and their dog, Neve. They enjoy taking long walks through the beautiful parks of the Pacific Northwest and creating delicious, nurturing food together.